CHARLES SPURGEON

40

MORNINGS &
EVENINGS IN
PSALMS

A 40-DAY DEVOTIONAL

WHITAKER
HOUSE

All Scripture quotations are taken from the King James Version of the Holy Bible.

Boldface type in the Scripture quotations indicates the author's emphasis.

40 MORNINGS AND EVENINGS IN PSALMS:
A 40-Day Devotional

ISBN: 978-1-64123-171-8
eBook ISBN: 978-1-64123-172-5
Printed in the United States of America
© 2018 by Whitaker House

Whitaker House
1030 Hunt Valley Circle
New Kensington, PA 15068
www.whitakerhouse.com

PREFACE

MORNINGS

Morning devotions anchor the soul, so that it will not very readily drift far away from God during the day. They perfume the heart so that it smells fragrant with piety until nightfall; they hold up the soul's garments so that it is less apt to stumble; they feed all their power so that the soul is not permitted to faint.

The morning is the gate of the day and should be well-guarded with prayer. It is one end of the thread on which the day's actions are strung and should be well-knit with devotion. If we felt the majesty of life more, we would be more careful of its mornings. He who rushes from his bed to his business and does not wait to worship is as foolish as if he had not put on his clothes or washed his face. He is as unwise as one who dashes into battle without being armed. Let us bathe in the softly flowing river of communion with God before the heat of the wilderness and the burden of the way begin to oppress us.

In writing these short reflections on the Psalms, I wanted to assist the believer in his or her private meditations. A child may sometimes console a desolate heart that might not otherwise have been cheered. Even a flower smiling upward from the ground may turn our thoughts heavenward. It is my hope that, by the Holy Spirit's grace, as the reader turns, morning by morning, to read a simple page, he will hear in it a still small voice that will speak the Word of God to his soul.

If there is not time to read both the morning devotional and a portion from Scripture, I earnestly request that this book would be set aside, for it would be a sore affliction to me to know that any family read the Word of God less on my account. I would be disappointed indeed if, after all, I frustrated my own purpose by diverting one moment of time to the perusal of my remarks that should have been given to searching the Word of God itself.

EVENINGS

When the noise and turmoil of the day are over, it is sweet to commune with God. The cool and calm of evening agree most delightfully with prayer and praise. The hours of the declining sun are like quiet alleys in the garden of time wherein man may find his Maker waiting to commune with him, even as of old the Lord God walked with Adam in paradise in the cool of the day.

It is fitting that we should set apart a peaceful season before the day has quite ended, a season of thanksgiving for abounding grace, of repentance for multiplied follies, of self-examination for insinuating evils. To leap from day to day like a mad hunter beating the bushes is an omen of being delivered over to destruction. But the solemn pause, the deliberate consideration—these are means of grace and signs of an indwelling life. The ocean tide stays awhile at ebb before it resolves to flood again; the moon sometimes lingers at its fullest size. There are distinct hedges in nature set between the seasons—even the strike of the bell is a little warning that men should not remove landmarks; instead, they should frequently examine the boundaries in their lives and keep up with due interval and solemnity the remembrance of the passing of days and months and years. Each evening it would be well to traverse the boundaries of the day and take note of all that it has brought and all that it has seen.

The reading of the Word and prayer are as gates of precious stones to admit us into the presence of the august Majesty. He is most blessed who most frequently swings those gates on their sapphire hinges. When the stars are revealed and all the hosts of heaven walk in golden glory, then surely that is the time when the solemn temple is lit up and the worshipper is invited to enter. If one hour can be endowed with a sacredness above the others, it must be the hour when the Lord looses the cords of Orion and leads forth the Bear and its cubs. (See Job 38:31–32.) Then voices from worlds afar call us to contemplation and adoration, and the stillness of the lower world prepares an oratory for the devout soul. He surely never prays at all who does not end the day as all men wish to end their lives—in prayer.

By this work, if I may lead one heart upward that otherwise would have drooped, or sow in a single mind a holy purpose that otherwise never would have been conceived, I will be grateful. May the Lord send us such results in thousands of instances, and His will be all the praise. The longer I live, the more deeply I am conscious that the Holy Spirit alone can make truth profitable to the heart; therefore, in earnest prayer, I commit this volume and its companion to His care.

—*Charles S. Spurgeon*

MORNING 1

I have exalted one chosen out of the people.
—Psalm 89:19

Why was Christ *"chosen out of the people"*? Speak, my heart, for heart-thoughts are best. Was it not that He might be able to be our Brother in the blessed tie of kindred blood? Oh, what relationship there is between Christ and the believer! The believer can say, "I have a Brother in heaven. I may be poor, but I have a Brother who is rich and is a King. Will He permit me to be in need while He is on His throne? Oh, no! He loves me; He is my Brother." Believer, wear this blessed thought like a diamond necklace around the neck of your memory. As a golden ring, put it on the finger of remembrance and use it as the King's own seal, stamping the petitions of your faith with the confidence of success. He is a *"brother...born for adversity"* (Proverbs 17:17); treat Him as such. Christ was also *"chosen out of the people"* so that He might know our needs and sympathize with us. He *"was in all points tempted like as we are, yet without sin"* (Hebrews 4:15). In all our sorrows, we have His sympathy. Temptation, pain, disappointment, weakness, weariness, poverty—He knows them all, for He has felt them all. Remember this, Christian, and let it comfort you. However difficult and painful your road may be, it is <u>marked by the footsteps</u> of your Savior. Even when you reach the dark valley of the shadow of death and the deep waters of the swelling <u>Jordan</u>, you will find His footprints there. In all places, wherever we go, He has been our forerunner; each burden we have to carry has once been laid on the shoulders of Emmanuel.

PS.139:5

Take courage! Royal feet have left a blood-red track on the road and consecrated the thorny path forever.

EVENING 1

Serve the LORD with gladness.
—Psalm 100:2

Delight in divine service is a token of acceptance. Those who serve God with a sad countenance, because they do what is unpleasant to them, are not serving Him at all; they bring the form of homage, but the life is absent. Our God requires no slaves to grace His throne. He is the Lord of the empire of love, and He would have His servants dressed in the uniform of joy. The angels of God serve Him with songs, not with groans. A murmur or a sigh would be mutiny in their ranks. Obedience that is not voluntary is disobedience, for the Lord looks at the heart, and if He sees that we serve Him from force, and not because we love Him, He will reject our offering. Service coupled with cheerfulness is heart-service and, therefore, true. Take away joyful willingness from the Christian, and you have removed the test of his sincerity. If a man is driven to battle, he is no patriot; but he who marches into the fray with flashing eye and beaming face, singing, "It is sweet to die for one's country," proves himself to be sincere in his patriotism. Cheerfulness is the support of our strength; in the joy of the Lord we are strong. It acts as the remover of difficulties. It is to our service what oil is to the wheels of a railroad car. Without oil the axle soon grows hot and accidents occur; if there is not a holy cheerfulness to oil our wheels, our spirits will be clogged with weariness. The man who is cheerful in his service to God proves that obedience is his element; he can sing,

> Make me to walk in Your commands,
> 'Tis a delightful road.

Reader, let me put this question to you: Do you *"serve the LORD with gladness"*? Let us show the people of the world, who think our religion is slavery, that to us, it is a delight and a joy! Let our gladness proclaim that we serve a good Master.

MORNING 2

Surely he shall deliver thee from the snare of the fowler.
—Psalm 91:3

God delivers His people *"from the snare of the fowler"* in two senses: *from* and *out of*. First, He delivers them *from* the snare; He does not let them enter it. Second, if they should be caught in it, He delivers them *out of* it. The first promise is the most precious to some; the second is the best to others. *"He shall deliver thee from the snare."* How? Trouble is often the means whereby God delivers us. God knows that our backsliding will soon end in our destruction, and, in mercy, He sends the rod. We say, "Lord, why is this happening?"—not knowing that our trouble has been the means of delivering us from far greater evil. Many have been thus saved from ruin by their sorrows and their crosses; these have frightened the birds from the net. At other times, God keeps His people from the snare of the fowler by giving them great spiritual strength, so that when they are tempted to do evil they say, *"How then can I do this great wickedness, and sin against God?"* (Genesis 39:9). But what a blessed thing it is that, if the believer does, in an evil hour, come into the net, God will bring him out of it!

O backslider, you may be cast down, but do not despair. Wanderer though you have been, hear what your Redeemer says: "Return, O backsliding children; I will have mercy on you." But you say you cannot return, for you are a captive. Then listen to the promise: *"Surely he shall deliver thee from the snare of the fowler."* You will yet be brought out of all evil into which you have fallen; and though you will never cease to repent of your ways, He who has loved you will not cast you away. He will receive you and give you joy and gladness, so *"that the bones which* [He has] *broken may rejoice"* (Psalm 51:8). No bird of paradise will die in the fowler's net.

EVENING 2

But I give myself unto prayer.
—Psalm 109:4

Lying tongues were busy against the reputation of David, but he did not defend himself; he moved the case to a higher court and pleaded before the great King Himself. Prayer is the safest method of replying to words of hatred. The psalmist did not pray in a cold-hearted manner; he gave himself to the exercise—threw his whole soul and heart into it—straining every sinew and muscle, as Jacob did when wrestling with the angel. (See Genesis 32:22–31.) In this way, and only in this way, will any of us speed to the throne of grace.

As a shadow has no power because there is no substance in it, even so, the supplication in which a man's proper self is not thoroughly present in agonizing earnestness and vehement desire is utterly ineffective, for it lacks that which would give it force. "Fervent prayer," said an old churchman, "like a cannon planted at the gates of heaven, makes them fly open."

The common fault with most of us is our readiness to yield to distractions. Our thoughts go roving here and there, and we make little progress toward our desired end. Like mercury, our minds will not hold together, but they roll off, this way and that. How great an evil this is! It injures us, and what is worse, it insults our God. What would we think of a petitioner, if, while having an audience with a prince, he played with a feather or tried to catch a fly?

Continuance and perseverance are intended in the expression of our text. David did not cry once and then relapse into silence; his holy clamor continued until it brought down the blessing. Prayer must not be our accidental work, but our daily business, our habit, and vocation. As artists give themselves to their models, and poets to their classical pursuits, so we too must addict ourselves to prayer. We must be immersed in prayer as in our element, and so *"pray without ceasing"* (1 Thessalonians 5:17). Lord, teach us to pray, that we may be more and more prevalent in supplication.

MORNING 3

They shall sing in the ways of the LORD.
—Psalm 138:5

Christians begin to *"sing in the ways of the* LORD*"* when they first lose their burdens at the foot of the cross. Not even the songs of the angels seem as sweet as the first song of rapture that gushes from the inner most soul of the forgiven child of God. You know how John Bunyan described it. He said that when poor Pilgrim lost his burden at the cross, he gave three great leaps and went on his way singing,

Blest Cross! blest Sepulchre! blest rather be
   The Man that there was put to shame for me!

Believer, do you remember the day when your fetters fell off? Do you remember the place where Jesus met you and said, *"'I have loved* [you] *with an everlasting love'* (Jeremiah 31:3) *'I have blotted out, as a thick cloud,* [your] *transgressions, and, as a cloud* [your] *sins'* (Isaiah 44:22). They will not be mentioned against you forevermore." Oh, what a sweet season it is when Jesus takes away the pain of sin!

When the Lord first pardoned my sin, I was so joyous that I could scarcely refrain from dancing. I thought, on my way home from the house where I had been set at liberty, that I must tell the stones in the street the story of my deliverance. My soul was so full of joy that I wanted to tell every snowflake that was falling from heaven of the wondrous love of Jesus, who had blotted out the sins of one of the chief of rebels. But it is not only at the beginning of the Christian life that believers have reason for song; as long as they live, they discover reasons to sing in the ways of the Lord, and their experience of His constant lovingkindness leads them to say, "*I will bless the Lord at all times: his praise shall continually be in my mouth*" (Psalm 34:1).

• See to it, friend, that you magnify the Lord this day.

EVENING 3

Turn away mine eyes from beholding vanity;
and quicken thou me in thy way.
—Psalm 119:37

There are various kinds of vanity. The cap and bells of the fool, the mirth of the world, the dance, the lyre, and the cup of the indulgent—all these things men know to be vanities. They display their proper name and title prominently. Far more treacherous are those equally conceited things: "*the cares of this world, and the deceitfulness of riches*" (Mark 4:19).

A person may follow vanity as much in his business as an actor seeks it in the theater. If he is spending his life in amassing wealth, he passes his days in a vain show. Unless we follow Christ and make God the great purpose of our lives, we differ only in appearance from the most frivolous. It is clear that there is much need of the first prayer of our text, "*Turn away mine eyes from beholding vanity.*" In the second prayer, "*Quicken thou me in thy way,*" the psalmist confessed that he was dull, heavy, lethargic, and all but dead.

Perhaps, dear reader, you feel the same. We are so sluggish that the best motives cannot quicken us, apart from the Lord Himself. What? Will not hell quicken me? Will I think of sinners perishing, and yet not be awakened? Will not heaven quicken me? Can I think of the reward that awaits the righteous and yet be cold? Will not death quicken me? Can I think of dying and standing before my God yet be slothful in my Master's service? Will not Christ's love constrain me? Can I think of His dear wounds, can I sit at the foot of His cross and not be stirred with fervency and zeal? It seems so!

No mere consideration can quicken us to zeal, but God Himself must do it; hence, the cry, "*Quicken **thou** me.*" The psalmist breathed out his whole soul in vehement pleadings; his body and his soul united in prayer. "*Turn away mine eyes,*" says the body. "*Quicken thou me,*" cries the soul. This is an appropriate prayer for every day.

O Lord, hear it in my case this night.

MORNING 4

*Thou hast made the LORD, which is my refuge,
even the most High, thy habitation.*
—Psalm 91:9

The Israelites in the wilderness were continually exposed to change. Whenever the pillar halted its motion, the tents were pitched. But tomorrow, before the morning sun had risen, the trumpet sounded, the ark was in motion, and the fiery, cloudy pillar was leading the way through the narrow gorges of the mountain, up the hillside, or along the arid waste of the wilderness. They had scarcely time to rest a little before they heard the sound of "Away! This is not your rest; you must still be journeying onward toward Canaan!" They never stayed in one place very long. Even wells and palm trees could not detain them, yet they had an abiding home in their God. His cloudy pillar was the supporting beam for their tents; its flame by night, their household fire. They must go onward from place to place, continually changing, never having time to settle and to say, "Now we are secure; in this place we will dwell." "Yet," said Moses, "though we are always changing, Lord, You have 'been our dwelling place in all generations' (Psalm 90:1)."

The Christian knows no change with regard to God. He may be rich today and poor tomorrow; he may be sickly today and well tomorrow; he may be in happiness today and distressed tomorrow, but there is no change with regard to his relationship to God. If He loved me yesterday, He loves me today. My unmoving mansion of rest is my blessed Lord. Let prospects be blighted; let hopes be blasted; let joy be withered; and let mildew destroy everything. I have lost nothing of what I have in God. He is *my strong habitation, whereunto I may continually resort* (Psalm 71:3).

❂ I am a pilgrim in the world, but at home in my God. In the earth, I wander, but in God, I dwell in a quiet habitation.

EVENING 4

Whereby they have made thee glad.
—Psalm 45:8

Who are the ones who are privileged to make the Savior glad? His church—His people. But is it possible? He makes us glad, but how can we make Him glad? By our love.

We think our love is so cold and so faint; indeed, we must sorrowfully confess it to be, but it is very sweet to Christ. Hear His own eulogy of that love in the golden Song of Solomon: *"How fair is thy love, my sister, my spouse! how much better is thy love than wine!"* (Song of Solomon 4:10). See, loving heart, how He delights in you.

When you lean your head on His bosom, you not only receive, but also give Him joy.

When you gaze with love on His all-glorious face, you not only obtain comfort, but also impart delight.

Our praise, too, gives Him joy—not the song of the lips alone, but the melody of the heart's deep gratitude.

Our gifts, too, are very pleasant to Him. He loves to see us lay our time, our talents, and our substance upon the altar, not for the value of what we give, but for the sake of the motive from which the gift springs. To Him, the lowly offerings of His saints are more acceptable than the thousands of offerings of gold and silver. Holiness is like frankincense and myrrh to Him. Forgive your enemy, and you make Christ glad. Distribute of your substance to the poor, and He rejoices.

Be the means of saving souls, and you give Him the opportunity to see the fruit of His soul's labors. Proclaim His gospel, and you are a sweet aroma to Him. Go among the ignorant and lift up the cross, and you have given Him honor.

It is in your power even now to break the alabaster box and pour the precious oil of joy upon His head, as did the woman of old, whose memorial is told to this day wherever the gospel is preached. Will you be backward then? Will you not perfume your beloved Lord with the myrrh, aloes, and cinnamon of your heart's praise? Yes, ivory palaces, you will hear the songs of the saints!

MORNING 5

My soul, wait thou only upon God;
for my expectation is from him.
—Psalm 62:5

It is the believer's privilege to use this language. If he is looking for anything from the world, it is a poor *"expectation"* indeed. But if he looks to God for the supply of his needs, whether in temporal or spiritual blessings, his expectation will not be a vain one. Constantly, he may draw from the bank of faith and have his needs supplied out of the riches of God's lovingkindness.

I know this: I would rather have God for my banker than all the Rothschilds. My Lord never fails to honor His promises. When we bring them to His throne, He never sends them back unanswered. Therefore, I will wait only at His door, for He always opens it with the hand of lavish grace.

At this hour I will try Him anew. But we have expectations beyond this life. We will die soon, and then, our *"expectation is from him."* Do we not expect that when we lie on the bed of sickness He will send angels to carry us to His bosom? We believe that when the pulse is faint and the heart beats heavily, some angelic messenger will stand and look with loving eyes on us, and whisper, "Sister spirit, come away!" As we approach the heavenly gate, we expect to hear the welcome invitation, *"Come, ye blessed of my Father, inherit the kingdom prepared for you from the foundation of the world"* (Matthew 25:34). We are expecting harps of gold and crowns of glory; we are hoping soon to be among the multitude of shining ones before the throne. We are looking forward and longing for the time when we will be like our glorious Lord, for *"we shall see him as he is"* (1 John 3:2).

Then, if these are your expectations, O my soul, live for God. Live with the desire and resolve to glorify Him from whom come all your supplies, and of whose grace in your election, redemption, and calling, it is that you have any *"expectation"* of coming glory.

EVENING 5

They shall be abundantly satisfied with the fatness of thy house; and thou shalt make them drink of the river of thy pleasures.
—Psalm 36:8

The queen of Sheba was amazed at the sumptuousness of Solomon's table. She was overwhelmed when she saw the provision of a single day. She marveled equally at the number of servants who feasted at the royal table. But what is this compared with the hospitality of the God of grace? Hundreds of thousands of His people are fed daily; hungry and thirsty, they bring large appetites with them to the banquet, but not one of them leaves unsatisfied. There is enough for each, enough for all, enough forevermore. Though the host that feeds at Jehovah's table is as countless as the stars of heaven, each one receives his or her portion of meat. Think how much grace one saint requires, so much that nothing but the Infinite One could supply him for one day; yet the Lord spreads His table, not for one, but for many saints; not for one day, but for many years; not for many years only, but for generation after generation.

Observe the full feasting spoken of in the text. The guests at mercy's banquet are satisfied—no, they are *"abundantly satisfied."* They are filled not with ordinary fare, but with *"fatness,"* the unique abundance of God's own house. Such feasting is guaranteed by a faithful promise to all those children of men who put their trust under the shadow of Jehovah's wings.

I once thought that if I could just get the leftover meat at God's back door of grace, I would be satisfied—like the woman who said, *"The dogs eat of the crumbs which fall from their masters' table"* (Matthew 15:27). But no child of God is ever served with scraps and leftovers. Like Mephibosheth, they all eat from the king's own table. In matters of grace, we all have Benjamin's portion; we all have many times more than we could have expected. Although our needs are great, we are often amazed at the marvelous abundance of grace that God gives to us to enjoy.

MORNING 6

In my prosperity I said, I shall never be moved.
—Psalm 30:6

"*Moab...settled on his lees, and hath not been emptied from vessel to vessel*" (Jeremiah 48:11). Give a man wealth. Let his ships bring home continually rich freights, and let the winds and waves appear to be his servants, to bear his vessels across the bosom of the mighty deep. Let his lands yield abundantly, and let the weather be propitious to his crops. Let uninterrupted success attend him. Let him stand among men as a successful merchant. Let him enjoy continued health, and allow him with braced nerve and brilliant eye to march through the world and live happily. Give him a buoyant spirit. Let him have a song perpetually on his lips. Let his eyes ever sparkle with joy—and the natural consequence of such an easy state to any man, even if he is the best Christian who has ever lived, will be presumption.

good chance of success

Even David said, "*I shall never be moved,*" and we are not better than David, nor half so good. Brother, beware of the smooth places of the way. If you are treading them, or if the way is rough, thank God for it. If God would always rock us in the cradle of prosperity; if we were always dandled on the knees of fortune; if we did not have some stain on the alabaster pillar; if there were not a few clouds in the sky; if we did not have some bitter drops in the wine of this life, we would become intoxicated with pleasure. We would dream we stand, and stand we would, but it would be on a pinnacle. Like a man asleep on the mast, each moment we would be in jeopardy.

move lightly up & down

We bless God, then, for our afflictions. We thank Him for our ups and downs. We extol His name for losses of property, for we feel that had He not chastened us thus, we might have become too secure. Continued worldly prosperity is a fiery trial.

EVENING 6

Stop the way against them that persecute me:
say unto my soul, I am thy salvation.
—Psalm 35:3

What does this sweet prayer teach me? It will be my evening's petition, but first let it serve as an instructive meditation. The text informs me that David had his doubts; otherwise, why would he pray, *"Say unto my soul, I am thy salvation,"* if he were not sometimes plagued with doubts and fears? Let me, then, be encouraged, for I am not the only saint who has to complain of weakness of faith. If David doubted, I do not need to conclude that I am not a Christian because I have doubts. The text reminds me that David was not content while he had doubts and fears. Instead, he went immediately to the mercy seat to pray for assurance, which he valued as much as fine gold. I, too, must seek an abiding sense of my acceptance in the Beloved. I must have no joy when His love is not shed abroad in my soul. When my Bridegroom is gone from me, my soul must and will fast.

I also learn that David knew where to obtain full assurance. He went to his God in prayer, crying, *"Say unto my soul, I am thy salvation.*" I must spend much time alone with God if I expect to have a clear sense of Jesus's love. If my prayers cease, my eye of faith will grow dim. Much in prayer, much in heaven; slow in prayer, slow in progress.

I notice that David would not be satisfied unless his assurance had a divine source. *"Say unto my soul."* Lord, please speak to me! Nothing short of a divine testimony in the soul will ever satisfy the true Christian. Moreover, David could not rest unless his assurance had a vivid personality about it. *"Say unto my soul, I am thy salvation."*

Lord, if You say this to all the saints, it would mean nothing, unless You said it to me. Lord, I have sinned; I do not deserve Your smile. I hardly dare to ask, but oh, say to my soul, even to my soul, *"I am thy salvation."* Let me have a present, personal, unfailing, indisputable sense that I am Yours and that You are mine.

MORNING 7

For I am a stranger with thee, and a sojourner,
as all my fathers were.
—Psalm 39:12

Lord, I am a stranger *with* You, but not *to* You. All my natural alienation from You, Your grace has effectively removed. Now, in fellowship with You, I walk through this sinful world as a pilgrim in a foreign country. Lord, You are a stranger in Your own world. Man forgets You, dishonors You, sets up new laws and alien customs, and does not know You. When Your dear Son came to His own, His own did not receive Him. (See John 1:11.) *"He was in the world, and the world was made by him, and the world knew him not"* (verse 10). Never was a foreigner considered as questionable a character as much as Your beloved Son was among His own people.

It is no surprise, then, if I, who live the life of Jesus, am a stranger here below. Lord, I would not be a citizen where Jesus was an alien. His pierced hand has loosened the cords that once bound my soul to earth, and now I find myself a stranger in the land. Among those with whom I dwell, my speech seems to these an outlandish tongue, my manners unusual, and my actions strange. A barbarian would be more at home among genteel society than I could ever be among the company of sinners.

But here is the sweetness of my lot: I am a stranger along with You. You are my fellow sufferer, my fellow pilgrim. Oh, what joy to be in such blessed society! My heart burns within me by the way when You speak to me, and though I am a sojourner, I am far more blessed than those who sit on thrones or dwell in their comfortable houses.

EVENING 7

It is better to trust in the LORD than to
put confidence in man.
—Psalm 118:8

Undoubtedly, the reader has been tried with the temptation to rely on things that are seen, instead of resting alone on the invisible God. Christians often look to man for help and counsel and mar the noble simplicity of their reliance on their God. Does this evening's portion meet the eye of a child of God who is anxious about earthly concerns? Then I would reason with him for a while.

You say that you trust in Jesus, and only in Jesus, for your salvation. Then why are you troubled? "Because of my great care," you answer. Is it not written, *"Cast thy burden upon the LORD"* (Psalm 55:22)? Does Scripture not also say, *"Be careful for nothing; but in every thing by prayer and supplication with thanksgiving let your requests be made known unto God"* (Philippians 4:6)?

Can you not trust God for your material needs? "Oh, I wish I could," you say. If you cannot trust God for earthly needs, how can you dare to trust Him for spiritual needs? Can you trust Him for your soul's redemption and not rely on Him for a few lesser mercies? Is God not enough for your needs, or is His all-sufficiency too limited? Do you need another eye besides the One who sees every secret thing? Is His heart faint? Is His arm weary? If so, then seek another God; but if He is infinite, omnipotent, faithful, true, and all-wise, why do you waste your time seeking another confidence? Why do you comb the earth to find another foundation, when God is strong enough to bear all the weight that you can ever build upon Him?

Christian, just as you would not dilute your wine with water, do not alloy the gold of your faith with the dross of human confidence. Wait only on God, and let your hope come from Him. Do not covet Jonah's gourd, but rest in Jonah's God. Let the sandy foundations of earthly trust be the choice of fools; but like the one who foresees the storm, build your house upon the Rock of Ages.

MORNING 8

O ye sons of men, how long will ye turn my glory into
shame? how long will ye love vanity,
and seek after leasing?
—Psalm 4:2

An instructive writer has made a sad list of the honors that the blinded people of Israel awarded to their long-expected King. First, they gave Him a procession of honor, in which Roman legionaries, Jewish priests, men, and women took part—He Himself bearing His cross. This is the triumph that the world awards to Him who comes to overthrow man's direst foes. Derisive shouts are His only acclamations and cruel taunts His only tributes of praise.

Next, they presented Him with the wine of honor. Instead of a golden cup of generous wine, they offered Him the criminal's stupefying death-draught, which He refused because He would preserve an uninjured taste wherewith to taste of death. Afterward, when He cried, *"I thirst"* (John 19:28), they gave Him vinegar mixed with gall, thrust to His mouth on a sponge. Oh, wretched, detestable inhospitality to the King's Son.

Third, He was provided with a guard of honor, who showed their esteem of Him by gambling over His garments, which they had seized as their booty. Such was the bodyguard of the adored of heaven—a quartet of brutal gamblers.

Then a throne of honor was found for Him on the bloody tree; no easier place of rest would rebellious men yield to their faithful Lord. The cross was, in fact, the full expression of the world's feeling toward Him. "There," they seemed to say, "Son of God, this is the manner in which God Himself should be treated, could we reach Him."

Finally, the title of honor was nominally "King of the Jews," but that the blinded nation distinctly repudiated, and really called Him "King of thieves," by preferring Barabbas, and by placing Jesus in the place of highest shame between two thieves.

His glory was thus, in all things, turned into shame by the sons of men, but it will yet gladden the eyes of saints and angels, world without end.

EVENING 8

I will take heed to my ways.
—Psalm 39:1

Fellow pilgrim, do not say in your heart, "I will go here and there, and I will not sin," for you are never so far from the danger of sinning as to boast of security. The road is very muddy; it will be hard to pick your path so as not to soil your garments. This world is full of corruption; you will need to watch often if, in handling it, you are to keep yourself clean. At every turn in the road, there is a thief ready to rob you of your jewels. There is a temptation in every blessing and a snare in every joy. If you ever reach heaven, it will be a miracle of divine grace to be ascribed entirely to your Father's power. Be on your guard.

When a man carries an explosive in his hands, he should be careful not to go near an open flame. You, too, must take care that you do not enter into temptation. Even your daily activities are sharp tools; you must watch how you handle them. There is nothing in this world to foster a Christian's faith, but everything tries to destroy it. How quick you should be to look to God so that He may keep you! Your prayer should be, "Hold me up, and I will be safe."

Having prayed, you must also watch; guard every thought, word, and action with holy jealousy. Do not expose yourselves unnecessarily to danger, but if you are called to go where the darts are flying, never venture forth without your shield. If, even once, the devil finds you without protection, he will rejoice that his hour of triumph has come, and he will soon make you fall down wounded by his arrows.

Though you cannot be slain, you can be wounded. Be sober; be vigilant. Danger may come in the hour when everything seems to be the most secure. Therefore, take heed to your ways, and pray diligently. No one ever fell into error through being too watchful. May the Holy Spirit guide us in all our ways so that we may always please the Lord.

MORNING 9

I am poured out like water,
and all my bones are out of joint.
—Psalm 22:14 ~ ¡

Did earth or heaven ever behold a sadder spectacle of woe? In soul and body, our Lord felt Himself to be weak, as water poured on the ground. The placing of the cross in its socket had shaken Him with great violence, had strained all the ligaments, pained every nerve, and more or less dislocated all His bones. Burdened with His own weight, the majestic Sufferer felt the strain increasing every moment of those six long hours. His sense of faintness and general weakness were overpowering, while to His own consciousness He became nothing but a mass of misery and swooning sickness.

When Daniel saw the great vision, he thus described his sensations, *"There remained no strength in me: for my comeliness was turned in me into corruption, and I retained no strength"* (Daniel 10:8). How much more faint must have been our greater Prophet when He saw the dread vision of the wrath of God and felt it in His own soul! To us, sensations such as our Lord endured would have been unbearable, and kind unconsciousness would have come to our rescue; but in His case, He was wounded and felt the sword; He drained the cup and tasted every drop.

As we kneel before our now ascended Savior's throne, let us remember well the way by which He prepared it as a throne of grace for us. Let us, in spirit, drink of His cup, so that we may be strengthened for our hour of heaviness, whenever it may come. In His natural body, every member suffered, and so must it be in the spiritual. But as out of all His grief and woes His body came forth uninjured to glory and power, even so will His spiritual body come through the furnace with not so much as the smell of fire on it.

EVENING 9

Keep back thy servant also from presumptuous sins.
—Psalm 19:13

Such was the prayer of David, the *"man after* [God's] *own heart"* (Acts 13:22). If holy David needed to pray this way, how much more do we, babes in grace, need to do so!

It is as if he said, "Keep me back, or I will rush headlong over the precipice of sin." Our evil natures, like an ill-tempered horse, are prone to run away. May the grace of God put the bridle on them and hold them in, so that we do not rush into mischief. What might the best of us not do if it were not for the boundaries that the Lord sets upon us both in providence and in grace?

The psalmist's prayer is directed against the worst form of sin—that which is done with deliberation and willfulness. Even the holiest need to be "kept back" from the vilest transgressions. It is a solemn thing to find the apostle Paul warning saints against the most loathsome sins: *"Mortify therefore your members which are upon the earth; fornication, uncleanness, inordinate affection, evil concupiscence, and covetousness, which is idolatry*" (Colossians 3:5). What! Do saints need to be warned against such sins as these? Yes, they do. The whitest robes, unless their purity is preserved by divine grace, will be defiled by the blackest spots.

Experienced Christian, do not boast in your experience; you will trip if you look away from Him who "*is able to keep you from falling*" (Jude 24). You whose love is fervent, whose faith is constant, whose hopes are bright, do not say, "We will never sin." Instead, cry, "*Lead us not into temptation*" (Matthew 6:13). There is enough kindling in the heart of the best of men to light a fire that will burn to the lowest hell, unless God quenches the sparks as they fall. Who would have dreamed that righteous Lot could have been found drunken and committing uncleanness? Hazael said, "*Is thy servant a dog, that he should do this great thing?*" (2 Kings 8:13). We are very likely to ask the same self-righteous question.

May infinite wisdom cure us of the foolishness of self-confidence.

MORNING 10

…my heart is like wax;
it is melted in the midst of my bowels.
—Psalm 22:14

Our blessed Lord experienced a terrible sinking and melting of soul. "*The spirit of a man will sustain his infirmity; but a wounded spirit who can bear?*" (Proverbs 18:14). Deep depression of spirit is the most grievous of all trials; all else is as nothing. Well might the suffering Savior cry to His God, *"Be not far from me"* (Ps. 71:12), for above all other seasons, a man needs his God when his heart is melted within him because of heaviness.

Believer, come near the cross this morning and humbly adore the King of Glory as having once been brought far lower, in mental distress and inward anguish, than anyone among us; and mark His fitness to become a faithful High Priest, who can *"be touched with the feeling of our infirmities"* (Hebrews 4:15). Especially let those of us whose sadness springs directly from the withdrawal of a present sense of our Father's love enter into near and intimate communion with Jesus. Let us not give way to despair, since through this dark room the Master has passed before us.

Our souls may sometimes long and faint, and thirst even to anguish, to behold the light of the Lord's countenance. At such times let us sustain ourselves with the sweet fact of the sympathy of our great High Priest. Our drops of sorrow may well be forgotten in the ocean of His grief, but how high should our love rise! Come in, O strong and deep love of Jesus, like the sea at the flood in spring tides. Cover all my powers, drown all my sins, wash out all my cares, lift up my earthbound soul, and float it right up to my Lord's feet. There let me lie, a poor broken shell, washed up by His love, having no virtue or value, only venturing to whisper to Him that if He will put His ear to me, He will hear within my heart faint echoes of the vast waves of His own love that have brought me where it is my delight to lie, even at His feet forever.

EVENING 10

They compassed me about like bees:
they are quenched as the fire of thorns:
for in the name of the LORD I will destroy them.
—Psalm 118:12

Our Lord Jesus, by His death, did not purchase a right to only a part of us, but to our entire being. In His crucifixion and death, He contemplated our entire sanctification—spirit, soul, and body—so that in this triple kingdom, He Himself might reign supreme without a rival. It is the business of the new-born nature that God has given to the regenerated to assert the rights of the Lord Jesus Christ.

My soul, since you are a child of God, you must conquer each part of yourself that is not submitted to Christ; you must surrender all your powers and passions to the silver scepter of Jesus's gracious reign. You must never be satisfied until He who is King by purchase becomes King by gracious coronation, and reigns supreme in your life. Seeing then that sin has no right to any part of us, we go about a good and lawful warfare when we seek, in the name of God, to drive it out. My body, you are a member of Christ. Will you tolerate your subjection to the prince of darkness?

My soul, Christ has suffered for your sins and redeemed you with His most precious blood. Will you permit your memory to become a storehouse of evil, or your passions to be firebrands of iniquity? Will you surrender your judgment to be perverted by error, or your will to be chained by sin? No, my soul, you are Christ's, and sin has no right to you. Be courageous concerning this, Christian!

❧ Do not be discouraged as though your spiritual enemies could never be destroyed. You are able to overcome them, though not in your own strength; the weakest of them would be too much for you in that. But you can and will overcome them through the blood of the Lamb. Do not ask, "How will I banish them, for they are greater and mightier than I?" but go to the strong for strength, wait humbly on God, and the mighty God of Jacob will surely come to your rescue. Then you will sing of victory through His grace.

MORNING 11

All they that see me laugh me to scorn:
they shoot out the lip, they shake the head.
—Psalm 22:7

Mockery was a great ingredient in our Lord's woe. Judas mocked Him in the garden; the chief priests and scribes laughed Him to scorn; Herod considered Him to be insignificant; the servants and the soldiers jeered at Him and brutally insulted Him; Pilate and his guards ridiculed His royalty; and on the tree all sorts of horrid jests and hideous taunts were hurled at Him.

Ridicule is always hard to bear, but when we are in intense pain, it is so heartless, so cruel, that it cuts us to the quick. Imagine the Savior crucified, racked with anguish far beyond all human comprehension, and then, picture that motley multitude, all wagging their heads or thrusting out their lips in bitter contempt of one poor suffering victim! Surely there must have been something more in the Crucified One than they could see; otherwise, such a great and mixed crowd would not unanimously have honored Him with such contempt. Was it not evil confessing, in the very moment of its greatest apparent triumph, that after all it could do no more than mock at that victorious goodness that was then reigning on the cross?

O Jesus, "*despised and rejected of men*" (Isaiah 53:3), how could You die for men who treated you so horribly? Herein is amazing love, divine love, yes, love beyond measure. We, too, have despised You in the days of our unregeneracy, and even since our new birth, we have set the world high in our hearts. Yet You bled to heal our wounds and died to give us life.

Oh, that we could set You on a glorious high throne in all men's hearts! We would ring out Your praises over land and sea until men would as universally adore You as once they unanimously rejected You.

EVENING 11

*Deliver me from bloodguiltiness, O God,
thou God of my salvation: and my tongue shall
sing aloud of thy righteousness.*
—Psalm 51:14

In this solemn confession, it is pleasing to observe that David plainly named his sin. He did not call it manslaughter or speak of it as an indiscretion by which an unfortunate accident occurred to a worthy man, but he called it by its true name: "*bloodguiltiness.*" He did not actually kill the husband of Bathsheba, but he planned in his heart that Uriah should be slain; therefore, he stood before the Lord as a murderer.

Learn in confession to be honest with God. Do not give fair names to foul sins; call them what you will, they will smell no sweeter. See your sins as God sees them; with all openness of heart, acknowledge their real character.

Observe that David was evidently oppressed with the heinousness of his sin. It is easy to use words, but it is harder to feel their meaning. The fifty-first psalm is the portrait of a contrite spirit. Let us seek to have the same brokenness of heart; for however excellent our words may be, if our hearts are not conscious that we are deserving of hell because of our sins, we cannot expect to find forgiveness.

Our text has in it an earnest prayer that is addressed to the God of salvation. It is His prerogative to forgive; it is His very name and nature to save those who seek His face. Better still, the text calls Him the "*God of my salvation.*" Yes, blessed is His name! While I am continuing to go to Him through Jesus's blood, I can rejoice in the "*God of my salvation.*"

The psalmist ended with a commendable vow: if God would deliver him, he would sing—no, more than that, he would "*sing aloud.*" Who can sing in any other style in the face of such great mercy! But notice the subject of the song: God's righteousness. We must sing of the finished work of a precious Savior; and he who knows the most of forgiving love will sing the loudest.

MORNING 12

My God, my God, why hast thou forsaken me?
why art thou so far from helping me,
and from the words of my roaring?
—Psalm 22:1

We here behold the Savior in the depth of His sorrows. No other place so well shows the grief of Christ as Calvary, and no other moment at Calvary is so full of agony as that in which His cry rends the air—*"My God, my God, why hast thou forsaken me?"* At this moment, physical weakness was united with acute mental torture from the shame and ignominy through which He had to pass. He suffered spiritual agony surpassing all expression, resulting from the departure of His Father's presence, unbearably heightening His grief. This was the black midnight of His horror. It was then that He descended into the abyss of suffering.

No man can enter into the full meaning of these words. Some of us think at times that we could cry, "My God, my God, why have You forsaken me?" There are seasons when the brightness of our Father's smile is eclipsed by clouds and darkness, but let us remember that God never really forsakes us. It is only an illusory forsaking with us, but in Christ's case, it was a real forsaking. We grieve at a little withdrawal of our Father's love; but the real turning away of God's face from His Son, who will calculate how deep the agony that it caused Him? In our case, our cry is often dictated by unbelief. In His case, it was the utterance of a dreadful fact, for God had really turned away from Him for a season.

O poor, distressed soul, who once lived in the sunshine of God's face, but are now in darkness, remember that He has not really forsaken you. God in the clouds is as much our God as when He shines forth in all the luster of His grace. But since even the thought that He has forsaken us gives us agony, what must the woe of the Savior have been when He exclaimed, *"My God, my God, why hast thou forsaken me?"*

EVENING 12

Yea, though I walk through the valley of the shadow of death, I will fear no evil: for thou art with me I will fear no evil: for thou art with me.
—Psalm 23:4

How independent of outward circumstances the Holy Spirit can make the Christian! What a bright light may shine within us when it is all dark without! How firm, how happy, how calm, how peaceful we may be, when the world shakes to and fro and the pillars of the earth are removed! Even death itself, with all its terrible influences, has no power to suspend the music of a Christian's heart. Instead, it makes that music become sweeter, clearer, and more heavenly, until the last kind act that death can do is to let the earthly strain melt into the heavenly chorus, the earthly joy into eternal bliss! Let us have confidence, then, in the blessed Spirit's power to comfort us.

Dear reader, are you facing poverty? Do not fear; the divine Spirit can give you, in your need, a greater abundance than the rich have in their wealth. You do not know what joys may be stored up for you in the cottage around which grace will plant the roses of content. Are you conscious of a growing failure of your bodily powers? Do you expect to suffer long nights of languishing and days of pain? Oh, do not be sad! That bed may become a throne to you. Little do you know how every pang that shoots through your body may be a refining fire to consume your dross—a beam of glory to light up the secret parts of your soul. Are your eyes growing dim? Jesus will be your light. Do your ears fail you? Jesus's name will be your soul's best music, and His person your dear delight. Socrates said, "Philosophers can be happy without music." Christians can be happier than philosophers when all outward causes of rejoicing are withdrawn.

In You, my God, my heart will triumph, come what may of troubles without! By Your power, O blessed Spirit, my heart will be exceedingly glad, though all things fail me here below.

MORNING 13

God, even our own God, shall bless us.
—Psalm 67:6

It is strange how little use we make of the spiritual blessings that God gives us, but it is stranger still how little use we make of God Himself. Though He is *our own God,* we apply ourselves but little to Him and ask but little of Him. How seldom do we ask counsel at the hands of the Lord! How often do we go about our business without seeking His guidance! In our troubles how constantly do we strive to bear our burdens ourselves, instead of casting them on the Lord, so that He may sustain us! This is not because we may not, for the Lord seems to say, "I am yours, soul. Come and make use of Me as you will. You may freely come to My store, and the more often, the more welcome."

It is our own fault if we do not avail ourselves of the riches of our God. Then, since you have such a Friend, and He invites you, draw from Him daily. Never be in need while you have God to go to. Never fear or faint while you have God to help you. Go to your Treasure and take whatever you need. There is all that you can desire. Learn the divine skill of making God all things to you. He can supply you with all, or, better still, He can be all to you. Let me urge you, then, to make use of your God. Make use of Him in prayer. Go to Him often, because He is *your* God. Oh, will you fail to use so great a privilege? Fly to Him, and tell Him all your needs. Use Him constantly—by faith—at all times.

If some dark circumstance has clouded your way, use your God as a light. If some strong enemy has attacked you, find in Jehovah a shield, "*for the LORD God is a sun and shield*" (Psalm 84:11) to His people. If you have lost your way in the mazes of life, use Him as a guide, for He will direct you. Whatever you are, and wherever you are, remember that God is just what you need and just where you need. He can do all you need.

EVENING 13

Thy gentleness hath made me great.
—Psalm 18:35

These last words may be translated, "Thy goodness hath made me great." David gratefully ascribed all his personal greatness not to his own goodness but to the goodness of God. "Thy providence" is another reading, and providence is nothing more than goodness in action. Goodness is the bud, and providence is the flower; goodness is the seed, and providence is the harvest. Some render it, "Thy help," which is another word for providence. Providence is the firm ally of the saints, aiding them in the service of their Lord. Two other renderings are, "Thy humility" and "Thy condescension hath made me great." The word *condescension* combines the ideas mentioned so far, including that of humility. The verse means that God's humbling of Himself is the cause of our being made great.

We are so little that if God would manifest His greatness without reaching out to us in love, we would be trampled under His feet. But God, who must stoop to view the skies and bow to see what angels do, lowers His eyes even further to look at the lowly and contrite and make them great. There are yet other translations. For instance, the Septuagint reads, "Thy discipline"—His fatherly correction—"hath made me great." The Chaldee paraphrase reads, "Thy word hath increased me."

The idea remains the same. David ascribed all his own greatness to the loving goodness of his Father in heaven. May this sentiment be echoed in our hearts this evening while we cast our crowns at Jesus's feet, and cry, *"Thy gentleness hath made me great."* How marvelous our experience of God's gentleness has been! How gentle are His corrections! How gentle His forbearance! How gentle His teachings! How gentle His entreaties! Meditate on this theme, believer. Let gratitude be awakened, let humility be deepened, and let love be rekindled before you fall asleep tonight.

● MORNING 14

Remember the word unto thy servant,
upon which thou hast caused me to hope.
—Psalm 119:49

NAMES OF
GOD P9 ▓
41

Whatever your special need may be, you may readily find some promise in the Bible suited to it. Are you faint and feeble because your way is rough and you are weary? Here is the promise: *"He giveth power to the faint"* (Isaiah 40:29). When you read such a promise, take it back to the great Promiser, and ask Him to fulfill His own Word.

Are you seeking after Christ and thirsting for closer communion with Him? This promise shines like a star on you: *"Blessed are they which do hunger and thirst after righteousness: for they shall be filled"* (Matthew 5:6). Take that promise to the throne continually; do not plead anything else, but go to God over and over again with this: "Lord, You have said it; do as You have said."

Are you distressed because of sin and burdened with the heavy load of your iniquities? Listen to these words: "*I, even I, am he that blotteth out thy transgressions for mine own sake, and will not remember thy sins*" (Isaiah 43:25). You have no merit of your own to plead for His pardon, but plead His written promises, and He will perform them.

Are you afraid lest you should not be able to hold on to the end, lest, after having thought yourself a child of God, you should prove a castaway? If that is your state, take this Word of grace to the throne and plead it: "*The mountains shall depart, and the hills be removed; but my kindness shall not depart from thee, neither shall the covenant of my peace be removed*" (Isaiah 54:10).

Feast your faith on God's own Word, and whatever your fears or needs, return to the <u>Bank of Faith</u> with your Father's note, saying, "*Remember the word unto thy servant, upon which thou hast caused me to hope.*"

EVENING 14

Look upon mine affliction and my pain;
and forgive all my sins.
—Psalm 25:18

It is well for us when prayers about our sorrows are linked with pleas concerning our sins—when, being under God's hand, we are not wholly absorbed with our pain, but remember our offenses against God. It is well, also, to take both sorrow and sin to the same place. It was to God that David carried his sorrow, and it was to God that David confessed his sin. Notice that we must take our sorrows to God. You may give even your little sorrows to God, for He counts the hairs of your head; your great sorrows you may commit to Him, for He holds the ocean in the hollow of His hand.

Go to Him, whatever your present trouble may be, and you will find Him willing and able to relieve you. But we must take our sins to God, too. We must carry them to the cross so that the blood may fall upon them, to purge away their guilt and to destroy their defiling power. The special lesson of the text is this: in the right spirit, we are to go to the Lord with our sorrows and our sins. Note that all David asked concerning his sorrow was, *"Look upon mine affliction and my pain."* But the next petition is vastly more precise, definite, decided, plain: *"Forgive all my sins."* Many sufferers would have put it, "Remove my affliction and my pain, and look at my sins." But David did not say this. He cried, "Lord, as for my affliction and my pain, I will not dictate to Your wisdom. Lord, look at them. I will leave them to You. I would be glad to have my pain removed, but do as You desire. But as for my sins, Lord, I know what I want to happen to them. I must have them forgiven; I cannot endure to lie under their curse for a moment longer."

A Christian considers sorrow to be lighter on the scale than sin; he can bear it if his troubles continue, but he cannot support the burden of his transgressions.

MORNING 15

Weeping may endure for a night,
but joy cometh in the morning.
—Psalm 30:5

Christian, if you are in a night of trial, think of tomorrow. Encourage your heart with thoughts of the coming of your Lord. Be patient, for He comes with clouds descending. Be patient! The Husbandman waits until He reaps His harvest. Be patient, for you know who has said, *"Behold, I come quickly; and my reward is with me, to give every man according as his work shall be"* (Revelation 22:12).

If you are distressed now, remember,

A few more rolling suns, at most,
   Will land you on fair Canaan's coast.

Your head may be crowned with thorny troubles now, but it will wear a starry crown before long. Your hand may be filled with cares now, but it will sweep the strings of the harp of heaven soon. Your garments may be soiled with dust now, but they will be white soon. Wait a little longer. Oh, how despicable our troubles and trials will seem when we look back on them! Looking at them here in the present, they seem immense; but when we get to heaven, we will then…

With transporting joys recount,
   The labors of our feet.

Our trials will then seem light and momentary afflictions.

Let us go on boldly. Even if the night is never so dark, the morning comes, which is more than they can say who are shut up in the darkness of hell. Do you know what it is thus to live on the future—to live on expectation—to anticipate heaven?

Happy believer, what joy it is to have so sure and so comforting a hope! It may be all dark now, but it will soon be light; it may be all trial now, but it will soon be all happiness. What does it matter though *"weeping may endure for a night,"* when *"joy cometh in the morning"*?

EVENING 15

Save thy people, and bless thine inheritance:
feed them also, and lift them up for ever.
—Psalm 28:9

God's people need lifting up. They are very heavy by nature. They have no wings, or, if they have, they are like the dove of old that lay among the pots; and they need divine grace to make them mount on wings covered with silver and feathers of yellow gold. By nature *"sparks fly upward"* (Job 5:7), but the sinful souls of men fall downward. O Lord, *"lift them up for ever"*!

There are three ways in which God's people need to be lifted up. They need to be elevated in character. Lift them up, O Lord; do not permit Your people to be like the world's people. The world lies in the wicked one; lift them out of it.

The world's people are looking after silver and gold, seeking their own pleasures and the gratification of their lusts; but, Lord, lift Your people up above all this. Keep them from being "muckrakers," as John Bunyan called the man who was always scraping after gold. Set their hearts upon their risen Lord and their heavenly heritage.

Moreover, believers need to be prospered in conflict. In battle, if they seem to fall, O Lord, be pleased to give them the victory. If the enemy's foot is upon their necks for a moment, help them to grasp the sword of the Spirit and eventually win the battle. Lord, lift up Your children's spirits in the day of conflict. Do not let them sit in the dust, mourning forever. Do not allow the adversary to vex them sorely and make them fret. But if they have been persecuted like Hannah (see 1 Samuel 1:2–20), let them sing of the mercy of a delivering God.

We may also ask our Lord to lift them up on the Last Day. Lift them up by taking them home, lift their bodies from the tomb, and raise their souls to Your eternal kingdom in glory.

MORNING 16

Shew thy marvellous lovingkindness, O thou that savest
by thy right hand them which put their trust in thee from
those that rise up against them.
—Psalm 17:7

When we give our hearts along with our charitable gifts, we give well, but we must often admit to failing in this respect.

Not so our Master and our Lord. His favors are always performed with the love of His heart. He does not send to us the cold meat and the broken pieces from the table of His luxury, but He dips our morsels into His own dish and seasons our provisions with the spices of His fragrant affections. When He puts the golden tokens of His grace into our palms, He accompanies the gift with such a warm pressure of our hand that the manner of His giving is as precious as the gift itself. He will come into our houses on His errands of kindness, but He will not act as some austere visitors do in a poor man's cottage; instead, He sits by our sides, not despising our poverty or blaming our weaknesses.

Beloved, with what smiles does He speak! What golden sentences drop from His gracious lips! What embraces of affection He bestows on us! If He had but given us pennies, the way of His giving would have gilded them; but as it is, the costly gifts are set in a golden basket by His pleasant carriage. It is impossible to doubt the sincerity of His charity, for there is a bleeding heart stamped on the face of all His benefactions. He gives *"liberally, and upbraideth not"* (James 1:5).

Not one hint that we are burdensome to Him; not one cold look for His poor pensioners; but He rejoices in His mercy and presses us to His bosom while He is pouring out His life for us. There is a fragrance in His spikenard that nothing but His heart could produce; there is a sweetness in His honeycomb that could not be in it unless the very essence of His soul's affection had been mingled with it. Oh, the rare communion that such singular sincerity produces! May we continually taste and know the blessedness of it!

EVENING 16

Thou shalt not be afraid for the terror by night.
—Psalm 91:5

What is this terror? It may be the cry of fire or the noise of thieves or imagined appearances or the shriek of sudden sickness or death. We live in the world of death and sorrow; therefore, we may look for trouble in the nighttime as well as during the glare of the broiling sun. Nor should this alarm us, for no matter what the terror is, the promise is that the believer will not be afraid. Why should he be fearful?

Let us make it more personal: why should *we* be afraid? God our Father is here, and He will be here all through the lonely hours. He is an almighty Watcher, a sleepless Guardian, a faithful Friend. Nothing can happen without His direction, for even hell itself is under His control. Darkness is not dark to Him. He has promised to be a wall of fire around His people: who can break through such a barrier? Unbelievers may well be afraid, for they have an angry God above them, a guilty conscience within them, and a yawning hell below them. But we who rest in Jesus are saved from all these through rich mercy. If we give way to foolish fear, we will dishonor our profession of faith and lead others to doubt the reality of godliness.

We ought to be afraid of being afraid, lest we vex the Holy Spirit by foolish distrust. Down, then, dismal foreboding and groundless apprehension. God has not forgotten to be gracious or shut up His tender mercies. It may be night in the soul, but there does not need to be any terror, for the God of love does not change. Children of light may walk through darkness, but they are not cast away. No, they are enabled to prove their adoption by trusting in their heavenly Father as hypocrites cannot do.

MORNING 17

He led them forth by the right way.
—Psalm 107:7

Uncertain experiences often lead the anxious believer to inquire, "Why is this happening to me?" I looked for light, but lo, darkness came; for peace, but found trouble. I said in my heart, my mountain stands firm; I will never be moved. Lord, you hide Your face, and I am troubled. It was but yesterday that I could read my title clear; today, my evidences are unsure and my hopes are clouded. Yesterday, I could climb to Pisgah's top and view the distant landscape. I could rejoice with confidence in my future inheritance. Today, my spirit has no hopes, but many fears; no joys, but much distress. Is this part of God's plan for me? Can this be the way in which God would bring me to heaven? Yes, it is even so.

The eclipse of your faith, the darkness of your mind, the fainting of your hope—all these things are but part of God's method of making you ready for the great inheritance into which you will soon enter. These trials are for the testing and strengthening of your faith. They are waves that wash you further upon the rock; they are winds that waft your ship the more swiftly toward the desired haven. According to David's words, so it might be said of you, *"He bringeth them unto their desired haven"* (Psalm 107:30).

By honor and dishonor, by evil report and by good report, by plenty and by poverty, by joy and by distress, by persecution and by peace, by all these things are the lives of your souls maintained, and by each of these are you helped on your way. Oh, believer, do not think that your sorrows are out of God's plan; they are necessary parts of it. *"We must through much tribulation enter into the kingdom of God"* (Acts 14:22). Learn, then, even to *"count it all joy when ye fall into divers temptations"* (James 1:2).

EVENING 17

The LORD is King for ever and ever.
—Psalm 10:16

Jesus Christ makes no despotic claim of divine right, for He is really and truly the Lord's anointed! *"It pleased the Father that in him should all fulness dwell"* (Colossians 1:19). God has given to Him all power and all authority. As the Son of Man, He is now Head over all things to His church, and He reigns over heaven, earth, and hell with the keys of life and death.

Certain princes have delighted to call themselves kings by the popular will, and certainly our Lord Jesus Christ is such in His church. If it could be put to the vote whether He should be King in the church, every believing heart would crown Him. Oh, that we could crown Him more gloriously than we do! We would consider no expense to be wasted that would glorify

Christ. Suffering would be pleasure, and loss would be gain, if thereby we could surround His brow with brighter crowns and make Him more glorious in the eyes of men and angels.

Yes, He shall reign. Long live the King! All hail to You, King Jesus! Go forth, virgin souls who love your Lord. Bow at His feet, and strew His way with the lilies of your love and the roses of your gratitude: "Bring forth the royal diadem, and crown Him Lord of all." Moreover, our Lord Jesus is King in Zion by right of conquest. He has taken and carried by storm the hearts of His people, and He has slain their enemies who held them in cruel bondage. In the Red Sea of His own blood, our Redeemer has drowned the Pharaoh of our sins. Will He not be King in Jeshurun? He has delivered us from the iron yoke and heavy curse of the law: shall not the Liberator be crowned?

We are His portion, whom He has taken out of the hand of the Amorite with His sword and with His bow. Who will snatch His conquest from His hand? All hail, King Jesus! We gladly acknowledge Your gentle reign! Rule in our hearts forever, lovely Prince of Peace.

MORNING 18

The LORD will perfect that which concerneth me: thy mercy, O LORD, endureth for ever.
—Psalm 138:8

> • THE LORD WILL — WORKOUT HIS PLANS FOR MY LIFE

Clearly, the confidence that the psalmist expressed here was a divine confidence. He did not say, "I have grace enough to perfect that which concerns me. My faith is so steady that it will not stagger. My love is so warm that it will never grow cold. My resolution is so firm that nothing can move it." No, his dependence was on the Lord alone. If we indulge in any confidence that is not grounded on the Rock of ages, our confidence is worse than a dream. It will fall on us and cover us with its ruins, to our sorrow and confusion.

All that nature spins, time will unravel, to the eternal confusion of all who are clothed therein. The psalmist was wise. He rested on nothing short of the Lord's work. It is the Lord who has begun the good work within us. It is He who has carried it on, and if He does not finish it, it will never be completed. If there is one stitch in the celestial garment of our righteousness that we are to insert ourselves, then we are lost; but this is our confidence: the Lord who began will perfect. He has done it all, must do it all, and will do it all. Our confidence must not be in what we have done or in what we have resolved to do, but entirely in what the Lord will do.

Unbelief insinuates, "You will never be able to stand. Look at the evil of your heart; you can never conquer sin. Remember the sinful pleasures and temptations of the world that besiege you; you will certainly be allured by them and led astray." Ah, yes, we would indeed perish if left to our own strength. If we had to navigate our frail vessels alone over so rough a sea, we might as well give up the voyage in despair. But thanks be to God! He *will perfect that which concerneth* [us]" and bring us to the *"desired haven"* (Psalm 107:30). We can never be too confident when we confide in Him alone, and never carry too many concerns when we have this assurance of His.

EVENING 18

For the LORD taketh pleasure in his people: he will
beautify the meek with salvation.
—Psalm 149:4

How comprehensive is the love of Jesus! There is no part of His people's interests that He does not consider, and there is nothing that concerns their welfare that is not important to Him. Not merely does He think of you, believer, as an immortal being, but as a mortal being, too. Do not deny it or doubt it: *"The very hairs of your head are all numbered"* (Matthew 10:30). *"The steps of a good man are ordered by the LORD: and he delighteth in his way"* (Psalm 37:23). It would be a sad thing for us if this mantle of love did not cover all our concerns, for what mischief might be worked in us in that part of our business that did not come under our gracious Lord's inspection!

Believer, rest assured that the heart of Jesus cares about your daily affairs. The breadth of His tender love is such that you may resort to Him in all matters; for in all your afflictions, He is afflicted, and as a father pities his children, so He pities you. The daily concerns of all His saints are borne in the broad heart of the Son of God. Oh, what a heart is His that does not merely understand His people but also comprehends the diverse and innumerable concerns of all those persons!

Do you think, O Christian, that you can measure the love of Christ? Think of what His love has brought you: justification, adoption, sanctification, eternal life! The riches of His goodness are unsearchable; you will never be able to name them or even conceive them. Oh, the breadth of the love of Christ! Will such a love as this have half our hearts? Will it have a cold love in return? Will Jesus's marvelous lovingkindness and tender care meet with but faint response and delayed acknowledgment?

Tune your harp, my soul, to a glad song of thanksgiving! Go to your rest rejoicing, for you are no desolate wanderer, but a beloved child, watched over, cared for, supplied, and defended by your Lord.

MORNING 19

Blessed be God, which hath not turned away my prayer,
nor his mercy from me.
—Psalm 66:20

In looking back on the character of our prayers, if we do it honestly, we will be filled with wonder that God has ever answered them. There may be some who think their prayers are worthy of acceptance—as the Pharisee did; but the true Christian, in a more enlightened retrospect, weeps over his prayers, and if he could retrace his steps, he would desire to pray more earnestly.

Remember, Christian, how cold your prayers have been. Instead of wrestling in prayer as Jacob did, your petitions have been weak and few—far removed from that humble, believing, persevering faith that cries, *"I will not let thee go, except thou bless me"* (Genesis 32:26). Yet, wonderful to say, God has heard these cold prayers of yours, and not only heard, but answered them.

Reflect also on how infrequent your prayers have been, unless you have been in trouble, and then, you have gone often to the mercy seat. But when deliverance has come, where has your constant supplication been? Yet, even though you have ceased to pray as you once did, God has not ceased to bless. When you have neglected the mercy seat, God has not deserted it, but the bright light of the Shekinah has always been visible between the wings of the cherubim.

Oh, it is marvelous that the Lord would regard those intermittent spasms of pleading that come and go with our needs. What a God He is to hear the prayers of those who come to Him when they have pressing needs, but neglect Him when they have received an answer; who approach Him when they are forced to come, but who almost forget to address Him when mercies are plentiful and sorrows are few!

Let His gracious kindness in hearing such prayers touch our hearts, so that we may from this point on be found *"praying always with all prayer and supplication in the Spirit"* (Ephesians 6:18).

EVENING 19

How precious also are thy thoughts unto me,
O God! how great is the sum of them!
—Psalm 139:17

Divine omniscience affords no comfort to the ungodly mind, but to the child of God it overflows with consolation. God is always thinking about us. He never turns aside His mind from us, and He always has us before His eyes. This is precisely as we would have it, for it would be dreadful to exist for a moment beyond the observation of our heavenly Father. His thoughts are always tender, loving, wise, prudent, and far-reaching. They bring to us countless benefits; therefore, it is a choice delight to remember them.

The Lord has always thought about His people: hence, their election and the covenant of grace by which their salvation is secured. He always will think about them: hence, their final perseverance by which they will be brought safely to their final rest. In all our wanderings, the vigilant gaze of the eternal Watcher is always fixed upon us; we never roam beyond the Shepherd's eye. In our sorrows, He observes us incessantly, and not one of our pains escapes His attention. In our toils, He marks all our weariness and writes in His book all the struggles of His faithful ones.

These thoughts of the Lord encompass us in all our paths and penetrate the innermost region of our being. Not a nerve or tissue, valve or vessel, of our bodily organization is uncared for; all the details of our little world are thought about by the great God. Dear reader, is this truth precious to you? Then hold to it. Never be led astray by those philosophic fools who preach an impersonal God and talk of self-existent, self-governing matter.

The Lord lives and thinks about us; this is a truth far too precious for us to be lightly robbed of it. The notice of a nobleman is valued so highly that he who has it counts his fortune made; but what is it to be thought of by the King of Kings! If the Lord thinks of us, all is well, and we may rejoice forevermore.

MORNING 20

Forsake me not,
O Lord: O my God, be not far from me.
—Psalm 38:21

Frequently, we pray that God would not forsake us in the hour of trial and temptation, but we too often forget that we need to use this prayer at all times. There is no moment of our lives, however holy, in which we can do without His constant upholding. Whether in light or in darkness, in communion or in temptation, we need the prayer, "*Forsake me not, O Lord.*' Hold me up, and I will be safe."

A little child, while learning to walk, always needs a mother's hand. The ship, left by the pilot, drifts at once from her course. We cannot do without continued aid from above. Let it, then, be your prayer today, "Do not forsake me, Father. Do not forsake Your child, lest he fall by the hand of the enemy. Shepherd, do not forsake Your lamb, lest he wander from the safety of the fold. Great Husbandman, do not forsake Your plant, lest it wither and die. '*Forsake me not, O Lord,*' now; and forsake me not at any moment of my life. Do not forsake me in my joys, lest they absorb my heart. Do not forsake me in my sorrows, lest I murmur against You. Do not forsake me in the day of my repentance, lest I lose the hope of pardon and fall into despair. Do not forsake me in the day of my strongest faith, lest faith degenerate into presumption. Do not forsake me, for without You I am weak, but with You I am strong. Do not forsake me, for my path is dangerous and full of snares, and

I cannot do without Your guidance. The hen does not forsake her brood; will You then cover me evermore with Your feathers and permit me to find my refuge under Your wings? *'Be not far from me; for trouble is near; for there is <u>none to help</u>'* (Psalm 22:11). *'Leave me not, neither forsake me, O God of my salvation'* (<u>Psalm 27:9</u>)."

EVENING 20

God is our refuge and strength,
a very present help in trouble.
—Psalm 46:1

Covenant blessings are not meant to be only looked at; they are intended to be appropriated. Even our Lord Jesus is given to us for our present use. Believer, do you make use of Christ as you should? When you are in trouble, why do you not tell Him all your grief? Does He not have a sympathizing heart, and can He not comfort and relieve you? No, you are going about to all your friends, except for your best Friend, and you are telling your tale everywhere except to the heart of your Lord.

Are you burdened with this day's sins? Here is a fountain filled with blood: use it, saint; use it. Has a sense of guilt returned to you? The pardoning grace of Jesus may be proved again and again. Come to Him at once for cleansing. Do you deplore your weakness? He is your strength; why not lean on Him? Do you feel naked? Come here, soul; put on the robe of Jesus's righteousness. Do not stand looking at it, but wear it.

Strip off your own righteousness and your own fears, too. Put on the fair white linen, for it was meant to wear.

Do you feel sick? Pull the night-bell of prayer, and call up the beloved Physician! He will give the medicine that will revive you. You are poor, but then you have *"a kinsman…, a mighty man of wealth"* (Ruth 2:1). Will you not go to Him and ask Him to give you of His abundance, when He has given you the promise that you will be a joint heir with Him?

All that He is and all that He has, He has made available to you. There is nothing Christ dislikes more than for His people to make a display of Him and not to use Him. He loves to be employed by us. The more burdens we put on His shoulders, the more precious He will be to us.

MORNING 21

Cast thy burden upon the LORD,
and he shall sustain thee.
—Psalm 55:22

Care, even though exercised on legitimate objects, if carried to excess, has in it the nature of sin. The precept to avoid anxious care is earnestly instilled by our Savior, again and again, in His teachings. It is reiterated by the apostles, and it is one that cannot be neglected without involving transgression: for the very essence of anxious care is the imagining that we are wiser than God, and the thrusting of ourselves into His place, to do for Him what He has undertaken to do for us.

We attempt to think of that which we imagine He will forget. We labor to take on ourselves our weary burden, as if He were unable or unwilling to take it for us. Now this disobedience to His plain precept, this unbelief in His Word, this presumption in intruding on His province, is all sinful. Yet more than this, anxious care often leads to acts of sin.

He who cannot calmly leave his affairs in God's hand, but will carry his own burden, is very likely to be tempted to use wrong means to help himself. This sin leads to a forsaking of God as our Counselor, resorting instead to human wisdom. This is going to the "*broken cisterns*" instead of to the "*fountain of living waters*" (Jeremiah 2:13)—a sin that was laid against ancient Israel.

Anxiety makes us doubt God's lovingkindness, and thus, our love for Him grows cold. We feel mistrust, and thus grieve the Spirit of God, so that our prayers become hindered, our consistent example marred, and our lives ones of self-seeking. Thus, lack of confidence in God leads us to wander far from Him; but if through simple faith in His promise, we cast each burden upon Him as it comes, and are "*careful for nothing*" (Philippians 4:6) because He undertakes to care for us, it will keep us close to Him and strengthen us against much temptation. "*Thou wilt keep him in perfect peace, whose mind is stayed on thee: because he trusteth in thee*" (Isaiah 26:3).

EVENING 21

Thou art my portion, O LORD:
I have said that I would keep thy words.
—Psalm 119:57

Look at your possessions, believer, and compare your portion with the lot of your fellowmen. Some make their living in the field. They are rich, and their harvests yield them a golden increase. But what are harvests compared with your God, who is the God of harvests? What are bursting granaries compared with Him, who is the Husbandman who feeds you with the bread of heaven? Some do their work in the city. Their wealth is abundant and flows to them in constant streams, until they become a very reservoir of gold. But what is gold compared with your God? You could not live on it; your spiritual life could not be sustained by it. Apply it to a troubled conscience, and could it reduce its pain? Apply it to a discouraged heart, and see if it could stop a single groan or lessen one's grief. But you have God, and in Him you have more than gold or riches could ever buy.

Some obtain their livelihood through that which most men love—applause and fame; but ask yourself, is God not more important to you than that? What if thousands of trumpets loudly blared your praise? Would this prepare you to cross the Jordan or cheer you in the face of judgment? No, there are griefs in life that wealth cannot alleviate; and there is the deep need at your dying hour for which no riches can provide.

But when you have God for your portion, you have more than all else put together. In Him every need is met, whether in life or in death. With God for your portion, you are rich indeed; for He will supply your needs, comfort your heart, assuage your grief, guide your steps, be with you in the dark valley, and then take you home to enjoy Him forever. *"I have enough"* (Genesis 33:9), Esau said; that statement is the best a worldly man can say. However, Jacob replied, "God hath dealt graciously with me, and…I have [all things, more than] *enough*" (Genesis 33:11), which is a note too high for carnal minds to understand.

MORNING 22

Thou lovest righteousness, and hatest wickedness:
therefore God, thy God, hath anointed thee with the oil
of gladness above thy fellows.
—Psalm 45:7

Be ye angry, and sin not" (Ephesians 4:26). There can hardly be goodness in a man if he is not angry at sin; he who loves truth must hate every false way. How our Lord Jesus hated it when the temptation came! Thrice it assailed Him in different forms, but He always met it with, "*Get thee behind me, Satan*" (Matthew 16:23; Mark 8:33; Luke 4:8). He hated sin in others—none the less fervently, because He showed His hate more often in tears of pity than in words of rebuke. Yet what language could be more stern, more Elijah-like, than the words, "*Woe unto you, scribes and Pharisees, hypocrites! for ye devour widows' houses, and for a pretence make long prayer*" (Matthew 23:14). He hated wickedness, so much that He bled to wound it to the heart; He died that it might die. He was buried that He might bury it in His tomb, and He rose that He might forever trample it beneath His feet.

Christ is in the gospel, and that gospel is opposed to wickedness in every shape. Wickedness arrays itself in fair garments and imitates the language of holiness; but the precepts of Jesus, like His famous scourge of small cords, chase it out of the temple and will not tolerate it in the church. So, too, in the heart where Jesus reigns, what war there is between Christ and Belial [the devil]! And when our Redeemer will come to be our Judge, those thundering words, "*Depart from me, ye cursed*" (Matthew 25:41), which are, indeed, but a prolongation of His life's teaching concerning sin, will manifest His abhorrence of iniquity.

As warm as His love is for sinners, so hot is His hatred of sin; as perfect as His righteousness is, so complete will be the destruction of every form of wickedness. O you glorious Champion of right and Destroyer of wrong, for this cause has God, even Your God, "*anointed thee with the oil of gladness above thy fellows*" (Psalm 45:7).

EVENING 22

Who forgiveth all thine iniquities;
who healeth all thy diseases.
—Psalm 103:3

Humbling as is the statement, yet the fact is certain that we are all more or less suffering under the disease of sin. What a comfort it is to know that we have a Great Physician who is both willing and able to heal us! Let us think about Him for a while tonight. His cures are very speedy; there is life in a look at Him. His cures are radical; He strikes at the center of the disease. Hence, His cures are sure and certain. He never fails, and the disease never returns.

❋ There is no relapse where Christ heals. There is no fear that His patients will be merely patched up for a season; He makes them new people. He gives them a new heart also and puts a right spirit within them. He is well skilled in all diseases. Physicians generally have some specialty. Although they may know a little about almost all our aches and pains, there is usually one area of medicine that they have studied above all others. But Jesus Christ is thoroughly acquainted with the whole of human nature. He is as much at home with one sinner as with another; never yet has He met with an out-of-the-way case that was difficult for Him. He has had extraordinary complications of strange diseases to deal with, but He has known exactly with one glance of His eye how to treat the patient. He is the only universal Doctor; and the medicine He gives is the only true remedy, healing in every instance.

Whatever our spiritual malady may be, we should go at once to this divine Physician. There is no brokenness of heart that Jesus cannot bind up. His blood *"cleanseth us from all sin"* (1 John 1:7). If we think of the countless number who have been delivered from all sorts of diseases through the power and virtue of His touch, we will joyfully put ourselves in His hands. We trust Him, and sin dies; we love Him, and grace lives; we wait for Him, and grace is strengthened; we see Him as He is, and grace is perfected forever.

MORNING 23

Ye that love the LORD, hate evil.
—Psalm 97:10

You have good reason to *"hate evil."* Consider what harm it has already brought you! Oh, what a world of mischief sin has brought into your heart! Sin blinded you so that you could not see the beauty of the Savior; it made you deaf so that you could not hear the Redeemer's tender invitations. Sin turned your feet into the way of death and poured poison into the very fountain of your being. It tainted your heart, and made it *"deceitful above all things, and desperately wicked"* (Jeremiah 17:9). Oh, what a creature you were when evil had done its utmost with you, before divine grace intervened! You were an heir of wrath even as others; you ran with the *"multitude to do evil"* (Exodus 23:2).

Such were all of us; but Paul reminded us: *"Ye are washed, but ye are sanctified, but ye are justified in the name of the Lord Jesus, and by the Spirit of our God"* (1 Corinthians 6:11). We have good reason, indeed, for hating evil when we look back and trace its deadly workings. Evil did such mischief to us that our souls would have been lost had not omnipotent love interfered to redeem us. Even now it is an active enemy, ever watching to do us harm and to drag us to perdition. Therefore *"hate evil,"* O Christians, unless you desire trouble. If you would strew your path with thorns and plant nettles on the pillow of your deathbed, then neglect to *"hate evil"*; but if you would live a happy life and die a peaceful death, then walk in all the ways of holiness, hating evil, even unto the end. If you truly love your Savior and would honor Him, then *"hate evil."*

We know of no cure for the love of evil in a Christian like abundant communion with the Lord Jesus. Dwell with Him, and it will be impossible for you to be at peace with sin.

EVENING 23

*There brake he the arrows of the bow, the shield, and the
sword, and the battle.*
—Psalm 76:3

Our Redeemer's glorious cry of *"It is finished"* (John 19:30)
was the death knell of all the adversaries of His people. It signi-
fied the breaking of *"the arrows of the bow, the shield, and the sword,
and the battle."* The Hero of Golgotha used His cross as an anvil
and His woes as a hammer, dashing to pieces bundle after bundle
of our sins, those poisoned *"arrows of the bow."* He trampled on
every indictment and destroyed every accusation. What glorious
blows the mighty Breaker gives with a hammer far weightier than
the fabled weapon of Thor! The diabolical darts were reduced
to fragments, and the infernal shields were broken like potters'
vessels! Jesus drew the dreadful sword of satanic power from its
sheath of hellish workmanship. He snapped it across His knee,
as a man breaks a bundle of dry wood and casts it into the fire.

Beloved, no sin of a believer can now be an arrow to wound
him mortally. No condemnation can now be a sword to kill
him, for the punishment of our sin was borne by Christ. A
full atonement was made for all our iniquities by our blessed
Substitute and Surety. Who can accuse us now? Who can condemn us? *"It is Christ that died, yea rather, that is risen again"*
(Romans 8:34). Jesus has emptied the quivers of hell, has
quenched every fiery dart, and has broken off the head of every
arrow of wrath. The ground is strewn with the splinters and
relics of the weapons of hell's warfare, which are visible to us

only to remind us of our former danger and of our great deliverance. Sin no longer has dominion over us. Jesus has made an end of it and put it away forever.

O enemy, your efforts to destroy have come to an end. Talk of all the wondrous works of the Lord. Make mention of His name, and do not keep silent either by day or when the sun goes to its rest at night. Bless the Lord, O my soul.

MORNING 24

The LORD hath done great things for us;
whereof we are glad.
— Psalm 126:3

Some Christians are sadly prone to look on the dark side of everything and to dwell more on what they have gone through than on what God has done for them. Ask for their impression of the Christian life, and they will describe their continual conflicts, their deep afflictions, their sad adversities, and the sinfulness of their hearts, yet with scarcely any allusion to the mercy and help that God has granted to them. But a Christian whose soul is in a healthy state will come forward joyously and say, "I will speak, not about myself, but to the honor of my God. *'He brought me up also out of an horrible pit, out of the miry clay, and set my feet upon a rock, and established my goings. And he hath put a new song in my mouth, even praise unto our God'* (Psalm 40:2–3). *'The LORD hath done great things for [me]; whereof [I am] glad.'*" Such an abstract of experience as this is the very best that any child of God can present.

It is true that we endure trials, but it is just as true that we are delivered out of them. It is true that we have our depravity, and mournfully do we know this, but it is quite as true that we have an all-sufficient Savior who overcomes these corruptions and delivers us from their dominion. In looking back, it would be wrong to deny that we have been in the Slough of Despond and have crept along the Valley of Humiliation, but it would be equally wicked to forget that we have been through them safely and profitably; we have not remained in them, thanks to our almighty Helper and Leader, who has brought *us out into a wealthy place* (Psalm 66:12).

The deeper our troubles, the louder our thanks to God, who has led us through all and preserved us until now. Our grief cannot mar the melody of our praise; we consider them to be the bass part of our lives' song, *"The LORD hath done great things for us; whereof we are glad."*

EVENING 24

The LORD is my light and my salvation; whom shall I
fear? the LORD is the strength of my life;
of whom shall I be afraid?
—Psalm 27:1

"The LORD is my light and my salvation." Here is personal interest: *"my light"* and *"my salvation."* The soul is assured of it and therefore declares it boldly. At the new birth, divine light is poured into the soul as the precursor of salvation; where there is not enough light to reveal our own darkness and to make us

long for the Lord Jesus, there is no evidence of salvation. After conversion, our God is our joy, comfort, guide, teacher, and in every sense our light. He is light within, light around, light reflected from us, and light to be revealed to us.

Notice that it is not said that the Lord merely gives light, but that He is light; nor that He gives salvation, but that He is salvation. He, then, who by faith lays hold upon God, has all covenant blessings in his possession. This truth established, the argument drawn from it is then put in the form of a question: *"Whom shall I fear?"* This question provides its own answer.

The powers of darkness are not to be feared, for the Lord, our light, destroys them. The damnation of hell is not to be dreaded, for the Lord is our salvation. This is a very different challenge from that of boastful Goliath. It rests not on the conceited strength of the *"arm of flesh"* (2 Chronicles 32:8), but on the real power of the omnipotent I Am. (See Exodus 3:14.) *"The Lord is the strength of my life."*

Here is a third glowing epithet; it shows that the writer's hope was fastened with a threefold cord that could not be broken. We may well accumulate terms of praise where the Lord lavishes deeds of grace. Our lives derive all their strength from God; if He deigns to make us strong, we cannot be weakened by all the schemes of the adversary. *"Of whom shall I be afraid?"* The bold question looks into the future as well as the present. *"If God be for us, who can be against us?"* (Romans 8:31)—either now or in the time to come!

MORNING 25

Delight thyself also in the LORD.
—Psalm 37:4

The teaching of these words must seem very surprising to those who are strangers to vital godliness; but to the sincere believer, it is only the communication of a recognized truth. The life of the believer is here described as a delight in God, and we are thus certified of the great fact that true faith overflows with happiness and joy. Ungodly persons and mere professors never look on faith as a joyful thing; to them it is service, duty, or necessity, but never pleasure or delight. If they attend to religion at all, it is either that they may gain thereby, or else because they dare not do otherwise.

The thought of delight in religion is so strange to most men that no two words in their language stand further apart than *holiness* and *delight*. But believers who know Christ understand that *delight* and *faith* are so blessedly united that the gates of hell cannot prevail to separate them. They who love God with all their hearts find that His *"ways are ways of pleasantness, and all* [His] *paths are peace"* (Proverbs 3:17). Such joys, such brimful delights, such overflowing blessedness do the saints discover in their Lord that so far from serving Him from custom, they would follow Him though all the world cast out His name as evil.

🍂 We do not fear God because of any compulsion. Our faith is no fetter; our profession is no bondage. We are neither dragged to holiness, nor driven to duty. No, our piety is our pleasure, our hope is our happiness, and our duty is our delight. *Delight* and *true religion* are as allied as root and flower—as indivisible as truth and certainty. They are, in fact, two precious jewels glittering side by side in a setting of gold.

EVENING 25

Unto thee will I cry, O LORD my rock; be not silent to me: lest, if thou be silent to me, I become like them that go down into the pit.
—Psalm 28:1

A cry is a natural expression of sorrow and a suitable utterance when all other modes of appeal fail us; but the cry must be directed to the Lord alone, for to cry to man is to waste our entreaties on the air. When we consider the readiness of the Lord to hear, and His ability to aid, we will see good reason for directing all our appeals immediately to the God of our salvation. It will be useless to call to the rocks to "*fall on us, and hide us*" (Revelation 6:16) in the Day of Judgment; but our Rock attends to our cries.

"*Be not silent to me.*" Those who go through merely the motions of prayer may be content without answers to their prayers, but genuine suppliants cannot be. They are not satisfied with the ability of prayer to calm the mind and subdue the will; they must go further and obtain actual replies from heaven, or they cannot rest. They long to receive those replies at once; they dread even a little of God's silence. God's voice is often so terrible that it shakes the wilderness, but His silence is equally terrible to an eager suppliant.

When God seems to close His ear, we must not close our mouths. Instead, we must cry with more earnestness. For when our note grows shrill with eagerness and grief, He will not deny us a hearing for long. What a dreadful situation we would be in if the Lord were to become forever silent to our prayers! *"Lest, if thou be silent to me, I become like them that go down into the pit."* Deprived of the God who answers prayer, we would be in a more pitiable plight than the dead in their graves and would soon sink to the same level as the lost in hell.

We *must* have answers to prayer. Ours is an urgent case of dire necessity. Surely the Lord will speak peace to our agitated minds, for He never can find it in His heart to permit His own elect to perish.

MORNING 26

Help, Lord; for the godly man ceaseth; for the faithful fail from among the children of men.
—Psalm 12:1

"Help, Lord." The prayer itself is remarkable, for it is short, but seasonable, concise, and suggestive. David mourned the scarcity of faithful men, and therefore lifted up his heart in supplication. When the creature failed, he flew to the Creator. He evidently felt his own weakness, or he would not have cried for help. At the same time, he intended honestly to exert

himself for the cause of truth, for the word "*help*" is inapplicable where we ourselves do nothing.

There is much directness, clearness of perception, and distinctness of utterance in this petition of two words—much more, indeed, than in the long rambling outpourings of certain professors. The psalmist runs directly to his God, with a well-considered prayer; he knows what he is seeking and where to seek it. Lord, teach us to pray in the same blessed manner.

PS. 22:11

The occasions for the use of this prayer are frequent. In providential afflictions, how suitable it is for tried believers who find all helpers failing them. Students, in doctrinal difficulties, may often obtain aid by lifting up this cry of "*Help, Lord*" to the Holy Spirit, the great Teacher. Spiritual warriors in inward conflicts may send to the throne for reinforcements, and this will be a model for their request. Workers in heavenly labor may thus obtain grace in time of need. Seeking sinners, in doubts and alarms, may offer up the same weighty supplication; in fact, in all these cases, times, and places, this will serve the turn of needy souls. "*Help, Lord,*" will suit us living and dying, suffering or laboring, rejoicing or sorrowing.

In Him, our help is found. Let us not be slack to cry to Him. The answer to the prayer is certain, if it is sincerely offered through Jesus. The Lord's character assures us that He will not leave His people. His relationship as Father and Husband guarantees us His aid. His gift of Jesus is a pledge of every good thing, and His sure promise stands, "*Fear not; I will help thee*" (Isaiah 41:13).

EVENING 26

*He that hath clean hands, and a pure heart; who hath
not lifted up his soul unto vanity, nor sworn deceitfully.*
—Psalm 24:4

Outward practical holiness is a very precious evidence of grace. It is to be feared that many who profess Christ have perverted the doctrine of justification by faith in such a way as to treat good works with contempt. Such people will receive everlasting contempt on the Last Great Day.

If our hands are not clean, let us wash them in Jesus's precious blood, so that we may lift up pure hands to God. *"Clean hands"* will not suffice unless they are connected with *"a pure heart."* True religion is a work of the heart. We may wash the outside of the cup and the plate as long as we please. However, if the inward parts are filthy, we are filthy altogether in the sight of God, for our hearts are more truly ourselves than are our hands.

The very life of our being lies in the inner nature, and that is why we have an imperative need for inward purity. It is the pure in heart who will see God; all others are but blind bats. The man who is born for heaven *"hath not lifted up his soul unto vanity."* All men have their joys by which their souls are lifted up. The worldly person lifts up his soul to carnal delights, which are mere empty vanities. However, the believer loves more substantial things. Like Jehoshaphat, he is lifted up in the ways of the Lord. He who is content with husks will be counted among the swine.

Does the world satisfy you? Then you have your reward and portion in this life; make much of it, for you will know no other joy. "*Nor sworn deceitfully.*" Believers in Christ are people of honor still. The Christian's word is his only oath; however, it is as good as the oaths of twenty others. False speaking will shut anyone out of heaven, for a liar will not enter into God's house, no matter what his profession of faith or deeds may be.

Reader, does today's text condemn you, or do you hope to "*ascend into the hill of the* LORD" (Psalm 24:3)?

MORNING 27

Thou art fairer than the children of men.
—Psalm 45:2

The entire person of Jesus is but as one gem, and His life is all along but one impression of the seal. He is altogether complete; not only in His several parts, but as a gracious, all-glorious whole. His character is not a mass of fair colors mixed confusedly, nor a heap of precious stones laid carelessly one upon another. He is a picture of beauty and a breastplate of glory. In Him, all the things of good repute are in their proper places and assist in adorning each other. Not one feature in His glorious person attracts attention at the expense of others, but He is perfectly and altogether lovely.

Oh, Jesus! Your power, Your grace, Your justice, Your tenderness, Your truth, Your majesty, and Your immutability make up such a man, or rather such a God-man, as neither heaven nor earth has seen elsewhere. Your infancy, Your eternity, Your sufferings, Your triumphs, Your death, and Your immortality are all woven in one gorgeous tapestry, without seam or rent. You are music without discord. You are many, and yet not divided. You are all things, and yet not diverse. As all the colors blend into one resplendent rainbow, so all the glories of heaven and earth meet in You and unite so wondrously that there is none like You in all things; if all the virtues of the most excellent were bound in one bundle, they could not rival You, mirror of all perfection. You have been anointed with the holy oil of myrrh and cassia, which Your God has reserved for You alone. As for Your fragrance, it is as the holy perfume, the like of which none other can ever mingle, even with the art of the apothecary; each spice is fragrant, but the compound is divine.

EVENING 27

Lead me in thy truth, and teach me: for thou art the
God of my salvation; on thee do I wait all the day.
—Psalm 25:5

When the believer has begun with trembling feet to walk in the way of the Lord, he still asks to be led onward like a little child upheld by his parent's helping hand, and he craves to be further instructed in the alphabet of truth.

Experiential instruction is the refrain of David's prayer in Psalm 25:4–5. David knew much, but he felt his ignorance and still desired to be in the Lord's school. Four times in these two verses he applied for a scholarship in the college of grace. It would be a good thing if believers would inquire into the good old ways of God's truth and earnestly ask the Holy Spirit to give them sanctified understanding and teachable spirits, instead of following their own devices and cutting out new paths of thought for themselves. *"For thou art the God of my salvation."*

The triune Jehovah is the Author and Perfecter of salvation for His people. Is He the God of your salvation? Do you find in the Father's election, in the Son's atonement, and in the Spirit's quickening, all the grounds of your eternal hopes? If so, you may use these means of grace as the basis for obtaining further blessings. If the Lord has ordained to save you, surely He will not refuse to instruct you in His ways.

It is a happy thing when we can address the Lord with the confidence that David manifested in our text; it gives us great power in prayer and comfort in trial. *"On thee do I wait all the day."* Patience is the fair handmaiden and daughter of faith; we cheerfully wait when we are certain that we will not wait in vain. It is our duty and privilege to wait on the Lord in service, in worship, in expectancy, and in trust all the days of our lives. Our faith will be tried faith; and if it is true faith, it will bear continued trial without yielding. We will not grow weary of waiting on God if we will remember how long and how graciously He once waited for us.

MORNING 28

Our heart shall rejoice in him,
because we have trusted in his holy name.
—Psalm 33:21

Blessed is the fact that Christians can rejoice even in the deepest distress. Although trouble may surround them, they still sing; and, like many birds, they sing best in their cages. The waves may roll over them, but their souls soon rise to the surface and see the light of God's countenance. They have a buoyancy about them that keeps their heads always above the water and helps them to sing amid the tempest, "God is with me still."

To whom will the glory be given? Oh, to Jesus—it is all by Jesus.

Trouble does not necessarily bring consolation with it to the believer, but the presence of the Son of God in the fiery furnace with him fills his heart with joy. He is sick and suffering, but Jesus visits him and makes his bed for him. He is dying, and the cold chilly waters of Jordan are gathering about him up to the neck, but Jesus puts His arms around him and cries, "Fear not, beloved; to die is to be blessed; the waters of death have their source in heaven. They are not bitter; they are sweet as nectar, for they flow from the throne of God." As the departing saint wades through the stream, and the billows gather around him, and heart and flesh fail him, the same voice sounds in his ears, *"Fear thou not; for I am with thee: be not dismayed; for I am thy God"* (Isaiah 41:10). As he nears the borders of the infinite unknown and is almost too afraid to enter the realm of shadows, Jesus says, *"Fear not, little flock; for it is your Father's good pleasure to give you the kingdom"* (Luke 12:32).

Thus strengthened and consoled, the believer is not afraid to die. He is even willing to depart, for since he has seen Jesus as the Morning Star, he longs to gaze on Him as the sun in its strength. Truly, the presence of Jesus is all the heaven we desire. He is at once "the glory of our brightest days; the comfort of our nights."

EVENING 28

When I cry unto thee, then shall mine enemies turn back: this I know; for God is for me.
—Psalm 56:9

It is impossible for any human words to express the full meaning of this delightful statement, *"God is for me."* He was for us before the universe was made. He was for us when He gave His well-beloved Son for us. He was for us when He struck the Only Begotten and laid the full weight of His wrath on Him; He was for us—though He was "against" Him. He was for us when we were ruined in the Fall; He loved us despite all. He was for us when we were rebels, defying Him with clenched fists. He was for us when He led us to humbly seek His face. He has been for us in many struggles; we have been summoned to encounter a multitude of dangers, and we have been assailed by internal and external temptations.

How could we have remained unharmed to this hour if He had not been for us? He is for us with the infinity of His being, the omnipotence of His love, and the infallibility of His wisdom. He is for us, arrayed in all His divine attributes. He is eternally and unchangeably for us. He will be for us when the blue skies are rolled up like a worn-out garment; He will be for us throughout eternity.

Because He is for us, our prayers will always secure His help. *"When I cry unto thee, then shall mine enemies turn back."* This is not an uncertain hope, but a well-grounded assurance: *"this I know."* I will direct my prayer to God and will look to Him for the answer, assured that it will come and that my enemies will be defeated, *"for God is for me."*

O believer, how happy you are with the King of Kings on your side! How safe you are with such a Protector! How sure is your cause, when it is pleaded by such an Advocate! *"If God be for us, who can be against us?"* (Romans 8:31).

MORNING 29

Bless the LORD, O my soul,
and forget not all his benefits.
—Psalm 103:2

It is a delightful and profitable occupation to mark the hand of God in the lives of ancient saints and to observe His goodness in delivering them, His mercy in pardoning them, and His faithfulness in keeping His covenant with them. But would it not be even more interesting and profitable for us to notice the hand of God in our own lives? Should we not look on our own history as being at least as full of God, as full of His goodness and of His truth, as much a proof of His faithfulness and veracity, as the lives of any of the saints who have gone before?

We do our Lord an injustice when we suppose that He wrought all His mighty acts and showed Himself strong for those in the early times, but does not perform wonders or "*bare his holy arm*" (Isaiah 52:10) for the saints who are now on the earth. Let us review our own lives. Surely in these we may discover some happy incidents, refreshing to ourselves and glorifying to our God. Have you had no deliverances? Have you passed through no rivers, supported by the divine presence? Have you walked through no fires unharmed? Have you had no manifestations? Have you had no choice favors? The God who gave Solomon the desire of his heart, has He never listened to you and answered your requests? That God of lavish bounty of whom David sang, "*Who satisfieth thy mouth with good things*" (Psalm 103:5), has He never satiated you with fatness? Have you never been made to lie down in green pastures? Have you never been led by the still waters?

Surely the goodness of God has been the same to us as to the saints of old. Let us, then, weave His mercies into a song. Let us take the pure gold of thankfulness and the jewels of praise and make them into another crown for the head of Jesus. Let our souls give forth music as sweet and as exhilarating as came from David's harp, while we praise the Lord whose mercy endures forever.

EVENING 29

Thou shalt arise, and have mercy upon Zion:
for the time to favour her, yea, the set time, is come.
For thy servants take pleasure in her stones,
and favour the dust thereof.
—Psalm 102:13–14

A selfish man in trouble is exceedingly hard to comfort, because the springs of his comfort lie entirely within himself; when he is sad, all his springs are dry. But a Christian who is full of love and generosity has other springs from which to supply himself with comfort besides those that lie within. First, he can go to God and find abundant help there; he can discover reasons for comfort in things relating to the world at large, to his country, and, above all, to the church.

David was exceedingly sorrowful in the psalm from which our text comes. He wrote, *"I am like an owl of the desert. I watch, and am as a sparrow alone upon the house top"* (Psalm 102:6–7). His only comfort was in the thought that God would *"arise, and have mercy upon Zion."* Even though David was sad, Zion would prosper. No matter how low his own condition was, Zion would arise.

Christian, learn to comfort yourself in God's gracious dealings toward the church. Should not what is so dear to your Master also be dear above all else to you? Even though your way may be dark, can you not encourage your heart with the triumphs of His cross and the advancement of His truth? Our own personal troubles will be forgotten when we look not only at what God has done and is doing for Zion, but also on the glorious things He will do for His church.

Believer, try this prescription whenever you are sad of heart and heavy in spirit: forget yourself and your little concerns, and seek the welfare and prosperity of Zion. When you bend your knee in prayer to God, do not limit your petition to the narrow circle of your own life, tried though it might be. Send out earnest prayers for the church's prosperity. *"Pray for the peace of Jerusalem"* (Psalm 122:6), and your own soul will be refreshed.

MORNING 30

* *So foolish was I, and ignorant:*
  I was as a beast before thee.
  —Psalm 73:22

Remember, this is the confession of the man after God's own heart; and in telling us his inner life, David wrote, *"So foolish was I, and ignorant."* The word *"foolish"* here means more than it signifies in everyday language. David, in the third verse of this psalm, wrote, *"I was envious at the foolish, when I saw the prosperity of the wicked,"* which shows that the folly he intended had sin in it. He put himself down as being *"foolish,"* and added a word that gave intensity to it, *"so foolish was I."* How foolish, he could not tell. It was a sinful folly, a folly that was not to be excused by frailty, but to be condemned because of its perverseness and willful ignorance; for he had been envious of the present prosperity of the ungodly and forgetful of the dreadful end awaiting them.

And are we better than David that we should call ourselves wise? Do we profess that we have attained perfection or that we have been so chastened that the rod has taken all our willfulness out of us? Ah, this is pride indeed! If David was foolish, how foolish would we be in our own esteem if we could but see ourselves!

Look back, believer. Think of your doubting God when He has been so faithful to you. Think of your foolish outcry of "Not so, my Father," when He crossed His hands in affliction to give you the larger blessing. Think of the many times when you have read His providences in the dark, misinterpreted His dispensations, and groaned out, "All these things are against me," when they are all working together for your good! Think how often you have chosen sin because of its pleasure, when indeed, that pleasure was a root of bitterness to you! Surely, if we know our own hearts, we must plead guilty to the indictment of a sinful folly.

Conscious of this "foolishness," we must make David's consequent resolve our own: *"Thou shalt guide me with thy counsel"* (Psalm 73:24).

EVENING 30

Why go I mourning?
—Psalm 42:9

Can you answer this question, believer? Can you find any reason why you are so often mourning instead of rejoicing?

Why yield to gloomy apprehension? Who told you that the night would never end in day? Who told you that the sea of circumstances would ebb out until there was nothing left but long, muddy stretches of horrible poverty? Who told you that the "winter of your discontent" would proceed from frost to frost; from snow, ice, and hail to deeper snow and an even worse blizzard of despair? Do you not know that day follows night, that flood comes after ebb, that spring and summer follow winter?

Then hope! Always hope, for God will not fail you. Do you not know that your God loves you in the midst of all your troubles? Mountains, when hidden in darkness, are as real as they are in daylight. In the same way, God's love is as true to you now as it was in your brightest moments. No father disciplines continuously.

Your Lord hates the rod as much as you do; He only cares to use it for the reason that should make you willing to receive it, namely, that it is for your lasting good. You will yet climb Jacob's ladder with the angels and behold Him who sits at the top of it—your covenant God. You will yet, amid the splendors of eternity, forget the trials of time—or only remember them to bless the God who led you through them and worked your lasting good by them.

Come and sing in the midst of tribulation. Rejoice even while you are passing through the furnace of affliction. Make the wilderness blossom like the rose. Cause the desert to ring with your exulting joys. These light afflictions will soon be over; then, forever with the Lord, your bliss will never diminish.

DAVID SAID —

Nevertheless I am continually with thee:
thou hast holden me by my right hand.
—Psalm 73:23

"*Nevertheless*"—notwithstanding all the foolishness and ignorance that David had just been confessing to God, not one atom the less was it true and certain that David was saved, accepted, and blessed by the constant presence of God. Fully conscious of his own lost state, and of the deceitfulness and vileness of his nature, yet, by a glorious outburst of faith, he sang, "*Nevertheless I am continually with thee.*"

Believer, you are forced to enter into the psalmist's confession and acknowledgment; endeavor in the same spirit to say, "Nevertheless, since I belong to Christ, I am continually with God!" This means that I am continually on His mind; He is always thinking of me for my good. I am continually before His eye; the eye of the Lord never sleeps, but is perpetually watching over my welfare. I am continually in His hand, so that none will be able to pluck me from it. I am continually on His heart, worn there as a memorial, even as the high priest bore the names of the twelve tribes on his heart forever.

You always think of me, O God. Your love continually reaches out to me. You are always making providence work for my good. You have set me as a signet on Your arm. Your love is as "*strong as death*" (Song of Solomon 8:6). "*Many waters cannot quench* [it], *neither can the floods drown it*" (verse 7). Surprising grace! You see me in Christ, and, though in myself abhorred, You behold me as wearing Christ's garments, washed in His blood; thus, I stand accepted in Your presence. I am continually in Your favor—*"continually with thee."*

Here is comfort for the tried and afflicted soul: vexed with the tempest within, look at the calm without. *"Nevertheless"*— Oh, say it in your heart, and take the peace it gives. *"Nevertheless I am continually with thee."*

EVENING 31

That he may set him with princes.
—Psalm 113:8

Our spiritual privileges are of the highest order. *"With princes"* is the place of select society. *"Truly our fellowship is with the Father, and with his Son Jesus Christ"* (1 John 1:3). Speaking of select society, there is none like this! *"Ye are a chosen generation, a royal priesthood,…a peculiar people"* (1 Peter 2:9). *"Ye are come unto…the general assembly and church of the firstborn, [whose names] are written in heaven"* (Hebrews 12:22–23). The saints have an audience with the King; princes have admittance to royalty, while common people must stand afar off. The child of God has free access to the inner courts of heaven. *"For through him we both have access by one Spirit unto the Father"* (Ephesians 2:18). *"Let us therefore come boldly,"* said the apostle, *"unto the throne of grace"* (Hebrews 4:16).

Among princes there is abundant wealth, but what is the abundance of princes compared to the riches of believers? *"For all things are yours;…and ye are Christ's; and Christ is God's"* (1 Corinthians 3:21, 23). *"He that spared not his own Son, but delivered him up for us all, how shall he not with him also freely give us all things?"* (Romans 8:32).

Princes have special power. A prince of heaven's empire has great influence; he wields a scepter in his own domain. He sits on Jesus's throne, for He *"hath made us kings and priests unto God"* (Revelation 1:6). We *"shall reign for ever and ever"* (Revelation 22:5). We reign over the united kingdom of time and eternity.

Princes also have special honor. We may look down upon all earthly dignity from the eminence upon which grace has placed us. For what is human grandeur to this: He *"hath raised us up together, and made us sit together in heavenly places in Christ Jesus"* (Ephesians 2:6)?

We share the honor of Christ. Compared to this, earthly splendors are not worth a thought. Communion with Jesus is a richer gem than any that ever glittered in a royal crown. Union with the Lord is a coronet of beauty outshining all the brilliance of imperial splendor.

MORNING 32

*The LORD reigneth; let the earth rejoice; let the
multitude of isles be glad thereof.*
—Psalm 97:1

There are no reasons for anxiety as long as today's blessed text is true. On earth, the Lord's power as readily controls the rage of the wicked as the rage of the sea. His love as easily refreshes the poor with mercy as the earth with showers. Majesty gleams in flashes of fire amid the tempest's horrors, and the glory of the Lord is seen in its grandeur in the fall of empires and the crash of thrones. In all our conflicts and tribulations, we may behold the hand of the divine King.

In hell, evil spirits acknowledge, with misery, His undoubted supremacy. When they are permitted to roam abroad, it is with a chain at their heels. The bit is in the mouth of the behemoth, and the hook in the jaws of the leviathan. Death's darts are under the Lord's lock, and the grave's prisons have divine power as their warden. The terrible vengeance of the Judge of all the earth makes fiends cower and tremble, even as dogs fear the hunter's whip.

In heaven, none doubt the sovereignty of the King Eternal, but all fall on their faces to pay Him homage. Angels are His courtiers, the redeemed His favorites, and all delight to serve Him, day and night. May we soon reach the city of the great King!

EVENING 32

Thou crownest the year with thy goodness.
—Psalm 65:11

All year round, every hour of every day, God is richly blessing us. Both when we are asleep and when we are awake,

His mercy attends us. The sun may not shine, but our God never ceases to shine on His children with beams of love. Like a river, His lovingkindness is always flowing with a fullness as inexhaustible as His own nature. Like the atmosphere that constantly surrounds the earth and is always ready to support the life of man, the benevolence of God surrounds all His creatures. In it, as in their element, they live, move, and have their being. As the sun on summer days makes us glad with rays that are warmer and brighter than at other times; as rivers are at certain seasons swollen by the rain; and as the atmosphere itself is sometimes fresher, more invigorating, or milder than previously, so it is with the mercy of God. It has its golden hours, its days of surplus, when the Lord magnifies His grace before the sons of men.

Among His blessings, the joyous days of harvest are a special season of abundant favor. It is the glory of autumn that the ripe gifts of providence are then abundantly bestowed. It is the season of realization, whereas all that came before was but hope and expectation. Great is the joy of harvest.

Happy are the reapers who fill their arms with the generosity of heaven. The psalmist tells us that the harvest is the crowning of the year. Surely these crowning mercies call for crowning thanksgiving! Let us offer thanks by inward expressions of gratitude.

Let our hearts be warmed. Let our spirits remember and meditate on the goodness of the Lord. Then let us praise Him, glorifying and magnifying His name, from whose bounty all this goodness flows. Let us glorify God by yielding our gifts to His purposes. A practical proof of our gratitude is a special thank offering to the <u>Lord of the harvest.</u>

MORNING 33

The trees of the LORD are full of sap;
The cedars of Lebanon, which he hath planted.
—Psalm 104:16

Lebanon's cedars are symbolic of the Christian, in that they owe their planting entirely to the Lord. This is quite true of every child of God. He is not man-planted or self-planted, but God-planted. The mysterious hand of the divine Spirit dropped the living seed into a heart that He had Himself prepared for its reception. Every true heir of heaven acknowledges the great Husbandman as his planter.

Moreover, the cedars of Lebanon are not dependent on man for their watering. They stand on the lofty rock, not moistened by human irrigation, yet our heavenly Father provides for them. Thus it is with the Christian who has learned to live by faith. He is independent of man, even in temporal things. For his continued maintenance, he looks to the Lord his God, and to Him alone. The dew of heaven is his portion, and the God of heaven is his fountain. Again, the cedars of Lebanon are not protected by any mortal power. They owe nothing to man for their preservation from stormy wind and tempest. They are God's trees, kept and preserved by Him, and by Him alone.

It is precisely the same with the Christian. He is not a hot-house plant, sheltered from temptation; he stands in the most exposed position. He has no shelter, no protection, except this: the broad wings of the eternal God always cover the cedars that He Himself has planted. Like cedars, believers are full of sap having vitality enough to always be green, even amid winter's snows.

Last, the flourishing and majestic condition of the cedar is to the praise of God only. The Lord, even the Lord alone, has been everything to the cedars; therefore, David very sweetly put it in one of the psalms, *"Praise the LORD from the earth… fruitful trees, and all cedars"* (Psalm 148:7, 9). In the believer, there is nothing that can magnify man. He is planted, nourished, and protected by the Lord's own hand, and to Him let all the glory be ascribed!

EVENING 33

> *Let the whole earth be filled with his glory;*
> *Amen, and Amen.*
> —Psalm 72:19

This is an enormous request. To intercede for a whole city requires us to stretch our faith, and there are times when prayer for one person is enough to stagger us. But how far-reaching was the psalmist's intercession! How comprehensive! How sublime! *"Let the whole earth be filled with his glory."* This prayer does not exempt a single country, no matter how crushed it may be by the foot of superstition. It does not exclude a single nation, no matter how barbarous it may be. This prayer was spoken for the cannibal as well as for the civilized person—for all regions and races. It encompasses the entire circumference of the earth and omits no child of Adam.

We must be up and doing for our Master, or we cannot honestly offer such a prayer. We are not praying this prayer with a sincere heart if we are not endeavoring, as God helps us, to extend the kingdom of our Master. Are there not some who neglect both intercession and work?

Reader, is the prayer of our text also your prayer? Turn your eyes to Calvary. See the Lord of Life nailed to the cross, with the crown of thorns on His brow, with His bleeding head, hands, and feet. What! Can you look upon this miracle of miracles—the death of the Son of God—without feeling within your heart a marvelous adoration that language could never express? When you perceive that the blood has been applied to your conscience and know that He has blotted out your sins, you are not a true believer unless you fall to your knees and cry out, "Let the whole earth be filled with his glory; Amen, and Amen."

How can you bow before the Crucified One in loving homage, then not wish to see your Monarch take His rightful place as Master of the world? Shame on you if you can pretend to love your Prince, but not desire to see Him as the Universal Ruler. Your piety is worthless unless it leads you to wish that the same mercy that has been extended to you may bless the whole world. Lord, it is harvest time. Put in Your sickle and reap.

MORNING 34

*Thou, Lord, hast made me glad through thy work: I
will triumph in the works of thy hands.*
—Psalm 92:4

Do you believe that your sins are forgiven and that Christ has made a full atonement for them? Then what a joyful Christian you ought to be! How you should live above the common trials and troubles of the world! Since sin is forgiven, can it matter what happens to you now? Luther said, "Smite, Lord, smite, for my sin is forgiven; if Thou hast but forgiven me, smite as hard as Thou wilt." In a similar spirit, you may say, "Send sickness, poverty, losses, crosses, persecution; send what You will, for You have forgiven me, and my soul is glad."

Christian, if you are thus saved, while you are glad, be grateful and loving. Cling to the cross that took your sin away; serve Him who served you. "*I beseech you therefore, brethren, by the mercies of God, that ye present your bodies a living sacrifice, holy, acceptable unto God, which is your reasonable service*" (Romans 12:1). Do not let your zeal evaporate in some little exuberant outburst of song. Show your love in expressive ways. Love the brethren of Him who loved you. If there is a Mephibosheth anywhere who is lame or halt, help him for Jonathan's sake. If there is a poor tried believer, weep with him and bear his cross for the sake of Him who wept for you and carried your sins. Since you are thus forgiven freely for Christ's sake, go and tell to others the joyful news of pardoning mercy. Do not be content with this unspeakable blessing for yourself alone, but publish abroad the story of the cross.

Holy gladness and holy boldness will make you a good preacher, and all the world will be a pulpit for you to preach in. Cheerful holiness is the most forcible of sermons, but the Lord must give it to you. Seek it this morning before you go into the world. When it is the Lord's work in which we rejoice, we do not need to be afraid of being too glad.

EVENING 34

Pull me out of the net that they have laid privily for me:
for thou art my strength.
—Psalm 31:4

Our spiritual enemies are of the same nature as the serpent in the garden of Eden; they seek to ensnare us by subtlety. The prayer of our text supposes the possibility of the believer being caught like a bird. So deftly does the fowler do his work that simple ones are soon surrounded by the net. The text asks that the captive one be delivered even out of Satan's meshes. This is a legitimate prayer, and one that can be granted. From between the jaws of the lion, and out of the belly of hell, eternal love can rescue the saint. A quick yank may be needed to save a believer from the net of temptation, and a mighty pull may be needed to extricate him from the snare of malicious cunning, but the Lord is equal to every emergency. The most skillfully placed nets of the hunter will never be able to hold His chosen ones. Those who are so clever at laying nets, those who tempt others, will themselves be destroyed.

"For thou art my strength." What inexpressible sweetness may be found in these few words! How joyfully we may encounter

struggles, and how cheerfully we may endure sufferings, when we can take hold of divine strength. Divine power will tear apart all the works of our enemies, confound their schemes, and frustrate their deceitful tricks. Happy is the one who has such matchless might engaged on his behalf! Our own strength is of little service when overwhelmed in the nets of base cunning, but the Lord's strength is always available to us. We only have to invoke it, and we will find it close at hand. If, by faith, we are depending on the strength of the mighty God of Israel alone, we may use our holy reliance as a plea in supplication.

MORNING 35

Give unto the LORD the glory due unto his name;
worship the LORD in the beauty of holiness.
—Psalm 29:2

God's glory is the result of His nature and acts. He is glorious in His character, for there is such a store of everything that is holy, good, and lovely in God that He must be glorious. The actions that flow from His character are also glorious; while He intends that they should manifest to His creatures His goodness, mercy, and justice, He is equally concerned that the glory associated with them should be given only to Himself. Nor is there anything in ourselves in which we may glory, for who makes us different from another? And what do we have that we did not receive from the God of all grace? Then how careful we should be to walk humbly before the Lord!

The moment we glorify ourselves, since there is room for one glory only in the universe, we set ourselves up as rivals of the Most High. Will the insect of an hour glorify itself against the sun that warmed it into life? Will pottery exalt itself above the one who fashioned it on the wheel? Will the dust of the desert strive with the whirlwind? Or the drops of the ocean struggle with the tempest? Give to the Lord, all righteous people. *"Give unto the LORD the glory due unto his name."*

Yet it is, perhaps, one of the hardest struggles of the Christian life to learn this sentence—*"Not unto us, O LORD, not unto us, but unto thy name give glory"* (Psalm 115:1). It is a lesson that God is ever teaching us, and teaching us sometimes through the most painful discipline. Let a Christian begin to boast, *"I can do all things,"* without adding *"through Christ which strengtheneth me"* (Philippians 4:13), and before long he will have to groan, "I can do nothing," and moan himself into the dust.

When we do anything for the Lord, and He is pleased to accept our actions, let us lay our crown at His feet and exclaim, *"Not I, but the grace of God which was with me"* (1 Corinthians 15:10)!

EVENING 35

Into thine hand I commit my spirit: thou hast redeemed me, O LORD God of truth.
—Psalm 31:5

Frequently, these words have been used by holy men and women in their hour of departure from this world. We will benefit from considering them this evening. The object of the faithful believer's concern in life and in death is not his body or his estate, but his spirit. His spirit is his most valuable treasure. If this is safe, all is well. What is the state of the body compared to the state of the spirit? The believer commits his spirit into the hands of God. It came from Him; it is His own. He has sustained it, and He is able to preserve it; it is most fitting that He should receive it.

All things are safe in Jehovah's hands. What we entrust to the Lord will be secure, both now and in that Day of days toward which we are quickly moving. It is peaceful living and glorious dying to rest in the care of heaven. At all times, we should commit our all to Jesus's faithful hands. Then, even though life may hang by a thread and adversities may multiply as the sands of the sea, our spirits will dwell at ease and delight in *"quiet resting places"* (Isaiah 32:18). *"Thou hast redeemed me, O LORD God of truth."*

Redemption is a solid basis for confidence. David did not know Calvary as we do, but temporal redemption comforted him. Will not eternal redemption comfort us even more sweetly? Past times of deliverance are strong pleas for present assistance. What the Lord has done in the past, He will do again, for He never changes. He is faithful to His promises and gracious to His saints. He will not turn away from His people.

MORNING 36

I am like a green olive tree in the house of God:
I trust in the mercy of God for ever and ever.
—Psalm 52:8

Meditate a little on this mercy of the Lord. It is *tender* mercy. With gentle, loving touch, He heals the broken in heart and binds up their wounds. He is as gracious in the manner of His mercy as in the matter of it. It is *great* mercy. There is nothing little in God. His mercy is like Himself: it is infinite. You cannot measure it. His mercy is so great that it forgives great sins to great sinners, after great lengths of time, and then, it gives great favors and great privileges, and raises us up to great enjoyments in the great heaven of the great God.

It is <u>undeserved</u> mercy, as indeed all true mercy must be, for deserved mercy is only a misnomer for justice. There was no right on the sinner's part to the kind consideration of the Most High. Had the rebel been doomed at once to eternal fire, he would have truly deserved the sentence. But if he was delivered from wrath, sovereign love alone was the reason, for there was no goodness in the sinner himself.

It is <u>rich</u> mercy. Some things are great, but have little efficacy in them, but this mercy is an encouragement to drooping spirits; a golden ointment to bleeding wounds; a heavenly bandage to broken bones; a royal chariot for weary feet; and an embrace of love for trembling hearts.

It is <u>manifold</u> mercy. As Bunyan said, "All the flowers in God's garden are double." There is no single mercy. You may think you have but one mercy, but you will find it to be a whole cluster of mercies.

It is <u>abounding</u> mercy. Millions have received it, yet far from its being exhausted, it is as fresh, as full, and as free as ever.

It is <u>unfailing</u> mercy. It will never leave you. If mercy is your friend, mercy will be with you in temptation to keep you from yielding; with you in trouble to prevent you from sinking; with you in living to be the light and life of your countenance; and with you in dying to be the joy of your soul when earthly comfort is ebbing fast.

EVENING 36

Trust in him at all times.
—Psalm 62:8

Faith is as much the rule of temporal life as it is of spiritual life. We ought to have faith in God for our earthly matters as well as for our heavenly concerns. It is only as we learn to trust in God to supply all our daily needs that we will live above the world. We are not to be idle, for that would show that we do not trust in God, who continually works, but in the devil, who is the father of idleness. We are not to be imprudent or rash, for that would be to trust chance rather than the living God, who is a God of economy and order. Acting in all prudence and uprightness, we are to rely simply and entirely on the Lord at all times.

Let me commend to you a life of trusting in God in temporal things. By trusting in God, you will not have to repent for having used sinful means to grow rich. Serve God with integrity. If you achieve no success, at least no sin will be on your conscience. By trusting in God, you will not become guilty of self-contradiction. He who trusts only in his own abilities sails this way today and that way the next, like a boat tossed about by the fickle wind. However, he who trusts in the Lord is like a steamship, which cuts through the waves, defies the wind, and makes one bright, silvery, straightforward track to her desired haven.

Be someone who has living principles within you. Never yield to the varying practices of worldly wisdom. Walk in the path of integrity with determined steps, and show that you are invincibly strong in the strength that confidence in God alone can provide. Thus you will be delivered from burdensome care. You will not be troubled by bad news. Your heart will be steadfast, "*trusting in the LORD*" (Psalm 112:7).

How pleasant it is to float along the stream of providence! There is no more blessed way of living than living a life of dependence upon a covenant-keeping God. We have no cares, "*for he careth for* [us]" (1 Peter 5:7). We have no troubles, because we cast our burdens upon the Lord.

MORNING 37

He sent redemption unto his people:
he hath commanded his covenant for ever:
holy and reverend is his name.
—Psalm 111:9

The Lord's people delight in the covenant. It is an unfailing source of consolation to them as often as the Holy Spirit leads them into its banqueting house and waves its banner of love. They delight to contemplate the antiquity of that covenant, remembering that before the sun knew its place or planets followed their orbits, the interests of the saints were made secure in Christ Jesus. It is particularly pleasing to them to remember the sureness of the covenant, while meditating on "*the sure mercies of David*" (Isaiah 55:3). They delight to celebrate it as signed, sealed, and ratified, in

DAVIDIC COVENANT - His seed would
be ruler over Israel, EVERLASTING

all things ordered well. It often makes their hearts swell with joy to think of its <u>immutability</u>, as a covenant that neither time nor eternity, life nor death, will ever be able to violate—a covenant as old as eternity and as everlasting as the Rock of ages.

They rejoice also to feast on the fullness of this covenant, for they see in it all things provided for them. God is their portion, Christ their Companion, the Spirit their Comforter, earth their house, and heaven their home. They see in it an inheritance reserved and assigned to every soul possessing an interest in its ancient and eternal gift. Their eyes sparkled when they saw it as a gold mine in the Bible; but oh, how their souls were gladdened when they saw in the last will and testament of their divine Kinsman that it was bequeathed to them!

More especially it is the pleasure of God's people to contemplate the graciousness of this covenant. They see that the law was made void because it was a covenant of works and depended on merit; but this they perceive to be enduring because grace is the basis, grace the condition, grace the strain, grace the bulwark, grace the foundation, grace the top-stone. The covenant is a treasury of wealth, a granary of food, a fountain of life, a storehouse of salvation, a charter of peace, and a haven of joy.

EVENING 37

The LORD trieth the righteous.
—Psalm 11:5

All events are under God's control. Consequently, all the trials of our outward lives may be directly traced to the great

kingdom. (ACTS 13:34)

First Cause. Out of the golden gate of God's ordinance, the armies of trial march forth in order, dressed in their iron armor and armed with weapons of war. All acts of God's providence are doors to trial. Even our mercies, like roses, have their thorns. Men may be drowned in seas of prosperity as well as in rivers of affliction. Our mountains are not too high and our valleys are not too low for temptations; trials lurk on all roads. Everywhere, above and beneath, we are surrounded and attacked by dangers. Yet no showers fall from the threatening clouds without permission; every drop has its order before it hurries to the earth.

The trials that come from God are sent to prove and strengthen our Christlike qualities. Therefore, at the same time, they illustrate the power of divine grace, test the genuineness of these qualities, and add to their effectiveness. Our Lord places so high a value on His people's faith that, in His infinite wisdom and abounding love, He will not screen them from the trials by which faith is strengthened. You would never have possessed the precious faith that now supports you if the trial of your faith had not been a trial by fire. You are a tree that never would have rooted as well if the winds of adversity had not rocked you back and forth and made you take firm hold of the precious truths of covenant grace.

Worldly ease is a great enemy to faith; it loosens the joints of holy valor and snaps the sinews of sacred courage. A hot-air balloon doesn't rise until the cords holding it to the earth are cut. Affliction does a similar service for believing souls. While the wheat sleeps comfortably in the husk, it is useless to man. It must be threshed out of its resting place before its value can be known. Thus it is good that Jehovah *"trieth the righteous,"* for their trials cause them to grow rich toward God.

MORNING 38

Have mercy upon me, O God, according to thy lovingkindness: according unto the multitude of thy tender mercies blot out my transgressions.
—Psalm 51:1

When the missionary Dr. William Carey was suffering from a serious illness, he was asked, "If this sickness should prove fatal, what passage would you select as the text for your funeral sermon?" He replied, "Oh, I feel that such a poor sinful creature is unworthy to have anything said about him, but if a funeral sermon must be preached, let it be from the words, *'Have mercy upon me, O God, according to thy lovingkindness: according unto the multitude of thy tender mercies blot out my transgressions.'"* In the same spirit of humility he directed in his will that the following inscription, and nothing more, should be cut on his gravestone:

WILLIAM CAREY, BORN AUGUST 17, 1761; DIED
A wretched, poor, and helpless worm,
On Thy kind arms I fall.

Only on the footing of free grace can the most experienced and most honored of the saints approach their God. The best of men are conscious above all others that they are men at best. Empty boats float high, but heavily laden vessels are low in the water; mere professors of faith can boast, but true children of God cry for mercy, recognizing their unworthiness.

We need the Lord's mercy on our good works, our prayers, our preaching, our almsgiving, and our holiest things. The blood was sprinkled not only on the doorposts of Israel's dwelling houses, but also on the sanctuary, the mercy seat, and the altar, because as sin intrudes into our holiest things, the blood of Jesus is needed to purify them from defilement. If mercy is needed to be exercised toward our duties, what will be said of our sins? How sweet to remember that inexhaustible mercy is waiting to be gracious to us, to restore our backslidings, and to make our broken bones rejoice!

EVENING 38

Lead me, O Lord, in thy righteousness because of mine enemies; make thy way straight before my face.
—Psalm 5:8

The enmity of the world against the followers of Christ is very bitter. People will forgive a thousand faults in others, but they will magnify the most trivial offenses in the followers of Jesus. Instead of regretting this state of affairs, which will accomplish nothing, let us use it for our benefit. Since so many are waiting for us to stumble, let this circumstance be our special motivation to walk very carefully before God.

If we live carelessly, the eagle-eyed world will soon see it. With its hundred tongues, it will spread the story, exaggerated and emblazoned by the zeal of slander. People will shout triumphantly, "Aha! We were right! See how these Christians act. They are all hypocrites!" In this way, much damage will be done to the cause of Christ, and His name will be gravely insulted. The cross of Christ is, in itself, an offense to the world. Let us be careful not to add any offense of our own. The cross is *"unto the Jews a stumblingblock"* (1 Corinthians 1:23). Let us make sure that we do not put any stumbling blocks where there are enough already. It is *"unto the Greeks foolishness"* (verse 23). Let us not add our folly, and thereby give any excuse for the scorn with which the worldly-wise deride the gospel.

How vigilant we need to be over ourselves! How strict we must be with our consciences! In the presence of adversaries who will misrepresent our best deeds and impugn our motives when they cannot censure our actions, how circumspect we must be! Pilgrims travel as suspect persons through Vanity Fair. Not only are we under surveillance, but also there are more spies than we imagine. The espionage is everywhere, at home and abroad. If we fall into our enemies' hands, we may sooner expect generosity from a wolf or mercy from a fiend than anything like patience with our weaknesses from men who spice their infidelity toward God with scandals against His people.

O Lord, lead us always, lest our enemies trip us up!

MORNING 39

Wait on the LORD: be of good courage,
and he shall strengthen thine heart.
—Psalm 27:14

It may seem to be an easy thing to wait, but it is one of the postures that a Christian soldier does not learn without years of teaching. <u>Marching</u> is much easier for God's warriors than standing still. There are hours of perplexity when the most willing spirit, anxiously desirous to serve the Lord, does not know what action to take. Then what will it do? Vex itself by despair? Fly back in cowardice, turn to the right hand in fear, or rush forward in presumption? No, it must simply wait. Wait in prayer, however.

Call on God, and spread the case before Him. Tell Him your difficulty and plead His promise of aid. In dilemmas between one duty and another, it is sweet to be humble as a child and to wait with simplicity of soul on the Lord. It is sure to be well with us when we feel and know our own folly and are heartily willing to be guided by the will of God. But wait in faith. Express your unstaggering confidence in Him. Unfaithful, untrusting waiting is an insult to the Lord. Believe that if He keep you tarrying even until midnight, He will come at the right time. The vision will come and will not tarry. Wait in quiet patience, not rebelling because you are under affliction, but blessing your God for it.

Never murmur as the children of Israel did against Moses. Never wish you could go back to the world again, but accept the situation as it is and put it as it stands, simply and with your whole heart, without any self-will, into the hand of your covenant God. Say, "Now, Lord, not my will, but Yours be done. I do not know what to do. I am brought to extremities, but I will wait until You divide the floods or drive back my foes.

I will wait, even if You keep me waiting for many days, because my heart is fixed on You alone, O God. My spirit waits for You in the full conviction that You will yet be my joy and my salvation, my refuge and my strong tower."

EVENING 39

I will sing of mercy and judgment:
unto thee, O LORD, will I sing.
—Psalm 101:1

Faith triumphs in trial. When reason is thrust into the inner prison, with her feet secured in the stocks, faith makes the dungeon walls ring with her joyful notes, as she cries, "*I will sing of mercy and judgment: unto thee, O LORD, will I sing*" (Psalm 101:1). Faith pulls the black mask from the face of trouble and discovers the angel underneath. Faith looks up at the cloud and sees that...

'Tis big with mercy and shall break
    In blessings on your head.

There is a theme for a song even in the judgments of God toward us. First, the trial is not as heavy as it might have been. Second, the trouble is not as severe as we deserve to bear. Third, our affliction is not as crushing as the burden that others have to carry.

Faith sees that even her worst sorrow is not given to her as a punishment. There is not a drop of God's wrath in it; it is all sent in love. Faith discerns love gleaming like a jewel on the breast of an angry God. Faith says of her grief, "This is a badge of honor, for the child must undergo the rod." Then she sings of the sweet result of her sorrows, because they are for her spiritual benefit. Faith says, *"Our light affliction, which is but for a moment, worketh for us a far more exceeding and eternal weight of glory"* (2 Corinthians 4:17). Therefore, Faith rides on its black horse, conquering and going forth to conquer, trampling down carnal reason and fleshly-mindedness, and singing songs of victory amid the thickest of the fray.

MORNING 40

> *Thou shalt guide me with thy counsel,*
> *and afterward receive me to glory.*
> —Psalm 73:24

The psalmist felt his <u>need of divine guidance</u>. He had just been discovering the foolishness of his own heart, and lest he would be constantly led astray by it, he resolved that God's counsel would henceforth guide him. A sense of our own folly is a great step toward being wise, when it leads us to <u>rely on the wisdom</u> of the Lord. The blind man leans on his friend's arm and reaches home in safety. Likewise, we should give ourselves up implicitly to divine guidance, nothing doubting, assured that though we cannot see, it is always safe to trust the all-seeing God.

"*Thou shalt*" is a blessed expression of confidence. He was sure that the Lord would not decline the condescending task.

There is a word for you, believer; rest in it. Be assured that your God will be your counselor and friend. He will guide you and will direct all your ways. In His written Word you have this assurance in part fulfilled, for Holy Scripture is His counsel to you.

We are happy to have God's Word always to guide us! What would the mariner be without his compass? And what would the Christian be without the Bible? This is the unerring chart, the map in which every <u>shoal</u> is described, and all the channels from the quicksands of destruction to the haven of salvation are mapped and marked by One who knows all the way. Bless You, O God, that we may trust You to guide us now, and guide us even to the end!

After this guidance through life, the psalmist anticipated a divine reception at last—*"and afterward receive me to glory."* What a thought for you, believer! God Himself will receive you to glory—you! Though you are wandering, erring, straying, yet He will bring you safe at last to glory! This is your portion. Live on it this day, and if perplexities should surround you, go, in the strength of this text, straight to the throne.

[handwritten margin note: PLACE OF STILL DARKNESS AFTER DEATH]

EVENING 40

The day is thine, the night also is thine.
—Psalm 74:16

Lord, You do not abdicate Your throne when the sun goes down, nor do You leave the world all through these long wintry nights to be the prey of evil. Your eyes watch us as the stars, and Your arms surround us as the zodiac encircles the sky. The dews of benevolent sleep and all the influences of the moon are in Your hand. The alarms and solemnities of night are the same with You. This is very sweet to me when watching through the midnight hours or when tossing to and fro in anguish.

There are precious fruits put forth by the moon as well as by the sun. May my Lord make me to be a favored partaker in them. The night of affliction is as much under the arrangement and control of the Lord of Love as the bright summer days when all is bliss. Jesus is in the tempest. His love wraps the night about itself as a mantle, but to the eye of faith, the sable robe is hardly a disguise. From the first watch of the night to the break of day, the eternal Watcher observes His saints. He overrules the shades and dews of midnight for His people's highest good. We believe in no rival deities of good and evil contending for mastery, but we hear the voice of Jehovah saying, "I create light, and I create darkness. I, the Lord, do all these things."

Gloomy seasons of religious indifference and social sin are not exempted from the divine purpose. When the altars of truth are defiled, and the ways of God forsaken, the Lord's servants weep with bitter sorrow. But they do not need to despair, for the darkest times are governed by the Lord, and they will come to their end at His command. What may seem defeat to us may be victory to Him.

ABOUT THE AUTHOR

CHARLES HADDON SPURGEON was born on June 19, 1834, at Kelvedon, Essex, England, the firstborn of eight surviving children. His parents were committed Christians, and his father was a preacher. Spurgeon was converted in 1850 at the age of fifteen. He began to help the poor and to hand out tracts, and he was known as "The Boy Preacher."

His next six years were eventful. He preached his first sermon at the age of sixteen. At age eighteen, he became the pastor of Waterbeach Baptist Chapel, preaching in a barn. Spurgeon preached over six hundred times before he reached the age of twenty. By 1854, he was well known and was asked to become the pastor of New Park Street Chapel in London. In 1856, Spurgeon married Susannah Thompson; they had twin sons, both of whom later entered the ministry.

Spurgeon's compelling sermons and lively preaching style drew multitudes of people, and many came to Christ. Soon, the crowds had grown so large that they blocked the narrow streets near the church. Services eventually had to be held in rented halls, and Spurgeon often preached to congregations of more than ten thousand. The Metropolitan Tabernacle was built in 1861 to accommodate the large numbers of people.

Spurgeon published over thirty-five hundred sermons, which were so popular that they sold by the ton. At one point, his sermons sold twenty-five thousand copies every week. An 1870 edition of the English magazine *Vanity Fair* called him an "original and powerful preacher...honest, resolute, sincere; lively, entertaining." The prime minister of England, members of the royal family, and Florence Nightingale, among others, went to hear him preach. Spurgeon preached to an estimated ten million people throughout his life. Not surprisingly, he is called the "Prince of Preachers."

In addition to his powerful preaching, Spurgeon founded and supported charitable outreaches, including educational institutions. His Pastors' College, which is still in existence today, taught nearly nine hundred students in Spurgeon's time. He also founded the famous Stockwell Orphanage.

Charles Spurgeon died in 1892, and his death was mourned by many.